Crystal Alchemy

A simple guide to activating and supporting an ascended consciousness, actualising human potential and lots of other stuff someone really should have told you.

~~~

http://michaelking.id.au
http://mysteryschool.org.au
http://facebook.com/crystalalchemy
http://youtube.com/cosmosismentoring

Copyright © 2012 Michael George King

Published by Vivid Publishing
P.O. Box 948, Fremantle
Western Australia 6959
www.vividpublishing.com.au

National Library of Australia Cataloguing-in-Publication data:
Author: King, Michael George.
Title: Crystal alchemy : a guide to supporting an ascended
            consciousness, seership and lots of other
            stuff someone really should have told you!
            / Michael George King.
ISBN: 9781922022448 (pbk.)
Subjects: Crystals--Psychic aspects.
            Precious stones--Psychic aspects.
            Spiritualism.
Dewey Number: 133.2548

Cover design and layout by Michael King
Cover photographs by Michael King
Illustrations by Miles Moody and Michael King
Compilation from lectures assistance by Patti McBain

All rights reserved. No part of this publication may be reproduced, stored in a retrieval system or transmitted in any form whatsoever, without the permission in writing from the author.

We wish to express our love and gratitude to all those seen and unseen who envision the Earth as a sphere of harmony and wisdom. We feel honoured to co-create with you to assist in the healing of humanity and our beloved Earth.

Michael King

Contents

Introduction

1   A short history of Alchemy

14   The Kingdoms of Nature

23   Crystals: Past, Present and Future

32   Sacredness, Respect, Wonder, Potential

43   Streams of Evolution and the Human Actualisation Process

62   Some of My Best Friends are Crystals

75   Crystal Clear

77   The Circle of Sirius

85   Attunement Meditation

94   Alchemical Healing Fundamentals

104 Chakra Balancing

112 Crystal Toolkit and Healing with Crystals

119 More working with Crystals

128 Planetary Healing and Rituals

147 The Cosmosis® Process

Conclusion

Foreword

~~~

Michael King lives an extraordinary life in an ordinary way. He endeavours to take all his experiences of life in, transform those experiences into love, and then radiate and express that love in every area of his life. He dedicates his life to the service behind the scenes of bringing new perspectives and solutions towards global harmony and enlightenment.

From an early age, Michael communed with the energies of nature, and has a natural rapport with them. In this book, Michael freely shares his love, knowledge, power and wisdom concerning the triggering of an alchemical awakening of dormant potential within us all through the use of crystals. Michael has a great love and respect for our planet Earth, and deeply appreciates the hardship she has undergone. Amongst his many roles he is the co-founder of the Insight Foundation. His life's work is expressed in the vision of the Cosmosis® Mentoring Centre –

"All life on Earth and beyond living in harmony and unity".

Reflections by Patti McBain, one of Michael's students

Introduction

~~~

When I was ten, my first dog, a terrier, was killed by accident one morning as Dad backed the car out of our driveway. I was devastated. Dad hadn't seen my little dog slip out the door with him as he left for work. A dog is an important part of a ten-year-old's life, so that afternoon Dad took me to the dog pound and Rastus decided she was coming home with me. She was part Chihuahua, part Corgi, with a round body and the sweetest face. We were told a policeman had found Rastus injured one day, and that he had nursed her back to health and then taken her to the pound.

Rastus quickly became my best buddy. She would come with us in the car when my Dad picked me up from school. One morning, a few years later, I was in our car parked outside my school sitting with Rastus and my Dad when a policeman walked by. Rastus went crazy. We had no idea why until the policeman came over. He was the one who had found and nursed her. She remembered him and was so happy to see him again!

The family who lived a few houses up from us also had a dog that Rastus would often play with over the ensuing years. One day, when I was fourteen, Rastus and I were playing outside. Rastus, true to style, decided to give our neighbour's dog some cheek and took off to chase it. I remember how helpless I felt that day, as I stood and watched a car come around our street corner. There wasn't even time to yell out as Rastus disappeared under the tyres… but my heart cried out.

I raced over and she just lay still on the road. She looked okay on the outside, but I knew on the inside she was hurt pretty bad. Dad carried her to our back-shed and sat with us for quite a while. I refused to leave Rastus. My heart was breaking as I watched her struggling for every breath. Dad knew she wouldn't make it and hunted me out of the shed. I took off into the bush behind our place. I spent a lot of my time in the bush. It was my private escape when life was going tough. I felt surrounded by the closeness of nature.

With anguish and the great love I felt for my friend dying in the shed, I boldly declared that I wanted to see whoever was in charge of "dog-ness". I called out with all my inner might for whoever it was that could do something to fix this.

Suddenly, I was totally dwarfed by this huge energy. I wasn't scared - I had always been sensitive to different nature energies in the bush and actually thought that was normal - but this energy was immense. I sensed it was 'the boss'. I demanded and pleaded with it to save my dog.

It responded, almost bewildered, "What for? What does it have to do with you?"

"But it is my dog and I love her!" I cried.

The energy then asked, "Who do you think you are that you can pick and choose what creatures live and die and the timing of those events? Creatures are prone to mechanical damage and this creature has suffered mechanical damage through its actions and the consequences are clear" it explained.

I felt chastised and realised that I was being selfish to hold onto her because I was emotionally attached. This energy helped me remember the cycle of nature and that life's events are really neither "good" nor "bad". This energy didn't have any judgment about Rastus dying, but it emanated immense unconditional love, pure acceptance and complete trust in the karma of choice and consequence. Through this encounter my anger and sadness were eased, but I still cried for my loss.

Years later, in my twenties, I was working in England when this energy reintroduced itself to me. I had by then started to put contemporary names to the different aspects of nature I had communed with all my life. I came to know this energy as 'Pan'.

***

I have collected rocks and crystals since I could walk. Over many years, I read about what crystals supposedly do and I don't pay attention to any of it. I just love the crystal, and see for myself what effect it has. I don't want to discourage you from experimenting, but I do want to discourage you from using books on crystals for anything other than a general guide. I have tried all sorts of things in crystal books and when I do exactly what it says to do, I just don't get repeatable results. I have found crystals don't do a lot of what people say they do. This is more to do with the mineral kingdom reacting differently to different people's energy fields rather than the books being technically incorrect. Having said that, the new age movement is full of 'wannabes' jumping on the bandwagon and spreading a lot of misinformation. The world is full of well-intentioned idiots, and sadly some not-so-well-intentioned ones too.

If you ask me what a certain mark on a crystal means, I will most likely reply that I don't know. I don't really care either. I read in books that one crystal is a record-keeper from Atlantis, and another crystal is a laser, and another is a something else.... But if I were to say to a crystal; "Hey, did you know that you are labelled a laser from Atlantis?" the crystal would say back to me "What is a label?"

The golden alchemical key to working with the natural energies is being without judgment and expectation. Since labels are all about both, let's just lose the labels right from the start. Two crystals can look identical as far as their facets, and one can be from Brazil and the other from Arkansas. They may share the same clarity and be a similar size, yet they will behave completely differently.

The potential within a crystal has much more to do with the energies prevailing whilst it was growing, and the consciousness it was exposed to during that period, rather than its shape.

Another important understanding to integrate is that once you reach the point in your spiritual growth process where the soul has merged with its personality - the third stage of human growth and development - and have started to consciously work with the indwelling spirit, which is who you truly are, then almost anything within the universe is available to you… if you know how to access it.

Any over-identification with something like numerology, astrology and 'crystalology' becomes yet another ridiculous self-imposed limitation. I see many otherwise highly developed humans justifying how they are: "I am an Aries, so I am like this". What complete nonsense! A spiritual initiate is not bound and conditioned by a planet's position when their physical body was built. Where is the mastery in that way of thinking?

Having said that, however, there are some generalities which may be concluded about the behaviour of crystals. For example, the clarity of a crystal tends to determine its ability to transmit or receive. A clearer, transparent crystal is more of a transmitter than a receiver, and is therefore masculinely-polarised. Likewise, a milky or cloudy crystal is more receptive than transmitting, and is therefore femininely-polarised. In addition, the more you work with a crystal and the more evolved it becomes through that interaction with you, so then does the indwelling elemental intelligence of the crystal become aware of what is outside its current limitation and its own planetary experience. Just as when you become aware of what is beyond the planet and beyond your physical senses, you can embody more potential and work within realms that are considered to be magical and even supernatural; so too is the experience for crystals, albeit upon a lower level of the evolutionary spiral.

Crystals are our friends. Working with crystals assists us to attune to the energy matrix of the Earth so that we can sustain higher frequencies, which may aid us in the actualisation of both our DNA and soul blueprints' fuller potential. They are a precious kingdom on this diverse planet, and we can work together with them to create more harmony amongst all the kingdoms. Such is the basic understanding, the mindset if you will, which is necessary to begin your journey for exploring crystal alchemy.

I embarked on a voyage of discovery to feel how crystals reacted with me. I found they knew what they were able to do. Over time, I developed my own understanding of crystal magic and developed/remembered an ancient approach to offer you, so you can start to experience the magic…and the key is…

"to love them."

In this book I will share with you an ancient alchemical understanding and view of the world, which will provide you with a lens into new knowing, new being and new awakenings. It is written in the style of the ancient initiate language, in that each page and paragraph is a collection of alchemical keys, which when pondered upon in the correct sequence shall initiate and activate the ancient knowing. …… If you but choose.

Michael King

Chapter 1
A short history of Alchemy

~~~

Alchemy is an influential philosophical tradition whose early practitioners' profound powers and insights were known from earliest times. The defining objectives of alchemy vary greatly in their purity of motive. They include the more materialistically-based creation of the fabled philosopher's stone - which supposedly possessed powers including the ability to turn base metals into the more noble metals such as gold or silver - to the altruistic motivation of creating the possibility of high-level creative Source being able to manifest in the earth plane for the betterment of humanity..... and everything in between.

Perhaps the most famous Alchemist of all time was Merlin the Enchanter, who helped Arthur create a utopian society for almost 50 years on an island off the Scottish coast about 1000 years ago. Camelot was founded and based upon advanced democratic principles. Its purpose was to seed into mass consciousness the potential of the democratic ideal, coupled with an ideology of human beings acting out of the service of love without being the slave of it. This ideal was held and actualised for long enough to create the potential for our modern democratic society. It allowed the evolution of modern political models and enabled a whole new potential for equality and opportunity, which is still being eventuated today. Such is the power of the collective enactment of new archetypal ideals. In fact, about every 1000 years a group of master souls incarnate on Earth together to enact such an ideal, either to create and live a new ideal in order to vivify it into the potential of future nows - like Camelot or Jesus' enactment 2000 years ago - or alternatively to enact the impact between mutually exclusive ideologies, so as to decide the path which the evolving civilisation shall take.

The latest such enactment in the mid-twentieth century was when Winston Churchill led the democratic coalition in opposition to the fascist alliance, which sought to plunge the planet into another dark age. The democratic and fascist ideals are mutually exclusive, so ultimately a clash between them was inevitable.

Alchemy, as we now understand it, was born in ancient Egypt way before recorded history, where the word Khem was used in reference to the fertility of the flood plains around the Nile. Egyptian beliefs in life after death, and the mummification procedures they developed, gave rise to rudimentary chemical knowledge and a goal of immortality. The premise was that if you could purify the human vessel of carnal energies and selfish desires, so then you could attain towards immortality. It was still common for high level spiritual initiates of the time to live for a thousand years or more, and the scientific study of what allowed such ones to seemingly cheat death gave birth to the science of Alchemy. There are actually many accounts of these long life spans even in the bible.

So it was actually the search for immortality which drove the study of matter and gave birth eventually to astrology, astronomy, cosmology, biology, medicine, chemistry and physics. Although these modern sciences took on a life of their own, down through the ages many have remained true to the original ideal of the early Alchemists, which was to purify/spiritualise the human vessel so that its spirit Source may descend into - and meld with - its human expression. Although the modern day ascension movement has its roots in ancient Alchemy, it has become perverted by becoming goal-oriented towards leaving the earth plane, rather than bringing spirit into the earth plane as was originally intended.

The spread of Alchemy.

By 332 BC, Alexander the Great had conquered Egypt. Greek philosophers became interested in the Egyptian ways. Greek views of how matter is made up of the four elements of nature - Fire, Earth, Air and Water - were merged with the Egyptian sacred science. The result was Khemia, the Greek word for Egypt. When Egypt was occupied by the Arabs in the 7th Century, they added 'al-' to the word Khemia, so 'al-khemia' is the origin of the modern word Alchemy. Much of the history of Alchemy sadly now exists only in an oral tradition and what may be accessed in the holographic records[1] of our planet.

Unfortunately more is not written about this early period in the history of Alchemy, because in 391 invading Christians burned the great library in Alexandria, destroying almost all relevant literary works.

Alchemists developed a framework of theory, terminology, experimental process and basic laboratory techniques that is still recognisable today. But alchemy differs

---

[1]. I shall not elaborate on the holographic records as they are part of the A,B,C's of esoteric study and anyone who selflessly and sincerely sets forth on this path will know of their existence beyond doubt. Every great spiritual tradition speaks of the planetary Hall of Records in one form or another. Even the Australian Aborigines have their 'Dreamtime'.

from modern science in the inclusion of Hermetic principles and practices related to metaphysics, ethics and spirituality.

In the eyes of the serious practitioner (as opposed to someone who approaches it as a form of superficial recreational spirituality, as most do), the heart of alchemy is spiritual. Transmutation of lead into gold is simply presented as an analogy for personal transmutation, purification, and perfection. Early alchemists, such as Zosimos of Panopolis (c. AD 300), highlighted the spiritual nature of the alchemical journey, symbolic of a spiritual regeneration and transformation of the human soul. This approach continued in the Middle Ages, as metaphysical aspects, substances, physical states, and material processes were used as metaphors for spiritual entities, spiritual states, and, ultimately, transformation. In this sense, the literal meanings of 'Alchemical Formulas' were 'blinds', hiding their true spiritual philosophy. Practitioners and patrons of alchemy such as Melchior Cibinensis and Pope Innocent VIII existed within the church of Rome, while Martin Luther applauded Alchemy for its authenticity and consistency with Christian teachings.

Alchemy was also developed independently in China by Taoist monks. The monks pursued the outer elixir of life - minerals, plants ... etc. - which could spiritualise the body and prolong life, and also the inner elixir of life, being the use of meditation and exercise techniques - such as Qigong - to manipulate the chi or life force of the body.

Like China and Egypt, India also developed Alchemy independently. They had beliefs similar to the Chinese, in that they used external and internal methods to purify the body and prolong life. In their alchemical work the Indians also invented steel, long before Bunsen and Kirchhoff's work, and they also realised the importance of flame colour in the identification of metals.

The introduction of Alchemy to the west came in the 8th Century when the Arabs brought it to Spain. This started a reaction which would eventually lead to a fundamental split of Alchemy into two paths, as it quickly spread to the rest of Europe. The Arabian belief was the beginnings of the scientific outlook, which was a very physical point of view, devoid of spirit. They only got part of the story from the Eastern Alchemists, which was mainly that metals are made up of mercury and sulphur in varying proportions. Gold was seen as the perfect metal and all others were less perfect; an idea popular among early western alchemists who 'jumped onto the bandwagon' so to speak. It was a very popular idea indeed, that these lower metals could be transmuted into gold by means of a substance known as the Philosopher's Stone. This was a partial truth, a falsehood which resulted from a purely physical perception of the art, rather than a holistic view which included an understanding of spiritual Source. Many so-called Alchemists propagated this understanding that they could turn base metals into gold for personal gain, whilst those who remained true to the Alchemical ideal of melding spirit with matter also encouraged this idea once they themselves began to be persecuted in Europe. The story that base metals could be transmuted into gold was used to gain protection and patronage from powerful individuals such as monarchs and clergy. This allowed them to continue their work within the intensely paranoid and superstitious period of times such as the inquisition. In Europe, Alchemy led to the discovery of manufacture of amalgams and advances in many other chemical processes and the apparatus required for them.

Eventually, by the 16th Century, the alchemists in Europe had separated into two distinct groups. The first group focussed on the discovery of new compounds and their reactions, properties and function - leading to what is now the sciences of medicine, chemistry, biology, metallurgy and physics. The second continued to look at the more spiritual, metaphysical side of alchemy, continuing the search for immortality and the transmutation of base human nature into its highest potential, so as to allow the fusion of the human being with its spiritual Source; to become the living spirit in human form. This second branch is the Alchemy that I teach. I term it 'Cosmosis® Personal Spiritual Alchemy'.

European Alchemy continued along these two lines all through the Renaissance. That era also saw a flourishing of con artists who would use chemical tricks and sleight of hand to "demonstrate" the transmutation of common metals into gold, or claim to possess secret knowledge that for a "small" initial investment they would share. These con artists persist to the present day and tend to give all Alchemists a bad name. The reality is that if it sounds too good to be true, it probably is!

It is important to emphasise that although there seem to be many branches of Alchemy, there are overlaps between all practitioners. Trying to classify them into wizards (alchemists), scientists (chemists, physicists), healers (medical practitioners both allopathic and natural) and craftsmen (metallurgists) is like attempting to sub-classify the various sides of a sphere. The demise of Western Alchemy was brought about by the rise of modern science, with its emphasis on rigorous quantitative experimentation and its disdain for "ancient wisdom". Although the seeds of these events were planted as early as the 17th century, Alchemy still thrived for another two hundred years. To my understanding though, all practitioners of the modern sciences are simply Alchemists of different flavours.

A deeper understanding

Alchemy is of historical interest in regards to science because it is the origin of modern chemistry and other branches of science. However, it is also of special interest to the historian of theology, because it is one of the foundations of the western esoteric tradition. The Alchemical tradition was, and still is, "both a way of life and an exercise of vision" as the great Alchemist Antoine Faivre put so eloquently. It is important to understand that the Earth's Alchemical traditions and expressions are not simply historical artefacts, but rather are dynamic, vital actualisations of the human spirit.

The greatest mistake you can make as you embark upon the study of Alchemy is to approach it within an existing framework of what you think you know. No preconceived notions, dogmas or doctrines concerning your understanding of the nature of reality will serve you in any way, other than to deny you true entry into the sacred Alchemical knowing. If you approach Alchemy from what you think you know, then all you will do is embed information, descriptions and labels into your mental body.

Alchemy is inherently about the synthesis of the intelligence of the heart with the intelligence of the mind. For that reason you must approach its study as a child approaches its investigation of its world.... with wonder and the freshness which comes from a lack of preconception. The methodological approach of modern science, which seeks to measure everything and to treat everything as mechanical in nature, will not allow you to enter into the mysteries of the universe of which Alchemy is the guardian and protector.

In order to draw upon the combined ancient knowing of all those who have penetrated into the mysteries of the nature of the universe, one must approach Spiritual Alchemy in terms of the perspective which gave rise to it. In a very real sense, the initial alchemical revelations come entirely from acknowledging the importance of just how different that perspective is from the one prevailing today. Nowadays, Alchemy is classed as merely an embryonic science - likened to a mechanical transformational technology like metallurgy - and this has veiled its true nature. Scientific it certainly was when it first reached the West some time late in the twelfth century, but in a thoroughly medieval sense, in which nothing - science least of all - could be separated from ethics, morals, and spirituality.

Practitioners of Spiritual Alchemy base its validity on the fact that they have themselves experienced transmutation, and have had visions or revelations that resulted in an experience of profound self-initiated personal transformation. Our reasoning is that one can only experience things that are real; and for us our personal experience of transformation is something that has integrity and it can and should be trusted. No faith is necessary as we have personally experienced the self-evident truth of our own living revelation. In short, experience provides us with both the criteria and the authority for making the claim that our Alchemical perspective is valid. In ages past this personal revelation posed a threat to existing religions of the time, and their system of blind faith, superstition and dogma could not possibly compete on equal terms. So, orthodox religion increasingly set about to eradicate and discredit Spiritual Alchemy.

In modern times, for most of the world's population, perspective - or our way of looking at the world - mostly performs a distancing function because we now live in a third-person society. Now our perspective tends to refer to a set of beliefs, doctrines, or philosophical ideas. However, when we speak of the Alchemists' perspective for which we claim validity, we do not mean that we merely hold a set of beliefs about the world, or that we merely accept a set of ideas concerning the world on an intellectual level. Rather, our Alchemical perspective is immediately derived from an actual first-person experience of the four intrinsic components which reveal the esoteric tradition to us, and render the esoteric perspective coherent in terms of our own unique experience. These four things are experienced as real, i.e. as deriving from the nature of reality itself. This Alchemical perspective gives rise to a unique and very specific experience of our world. That experience of the world not only gives rise to understanding, insight and wisdom, but also supports a deep knowing that is both consistent and congruent with the Alchemical perspective itself. Theory and practice are inextricably woven together. This is why the materials of Spiritual Alchemy indeed constitute a system of processes and of techniques of illumination which must be entered into as a permanent lifestyle. The Alchemical training I offer, termed Cosmosis®, has been formulated with the intention of making accessible to others a way of being in the world, which creates within your life a mode of transmitting gnosis (spiritual knowledge in the context of mystical enlightenment). In short, the spiritual Alchemist is an initiate, one "who knows."

Cosmosis® Personal Alchemical work has three stages:.

1. Know thyself: the preparatory stage when the Alchemist must confront unknown, chaotic material within themselves, to encounter the unilluminated aspects within and enlighten them.
2. The transcension of duality within oneself: By imposing transcendent norms upon seemingly opposing polarities, one learns to master the nature of reality as simply an infinite scale of vibrational expression from infinity to unity.
3. The systematic investigation into one's own universal and cosmic origins, and the subsequent revelation of Source.

Alchemy is alive and well in all its forms and expressions. One day soon, we will all realise this and it will be a great unifying revelation for the planet. It will lead to a new intensity of combined effort towards the betterment of humanity, and I hope I live to see that in my lifetime.

In the final analysis, if you are serious about Personal Spiritual Alchemy.... find someone a few steps ahead of you on that path, one who walks the talk and is able to demonstrate some degree of mastery, and take instruction!

Chapter 2
The Kingdoms of Nature

~~~

The densest level of consciousness within the kingdoms of nature on our beloved Earth is the mineral kingdom. The mineral kingdom is constituted of elements which are the various building blocks of form in different configurations, different sizes and different properties - as you perhaps remember from your chemistry periodic table at school. Pairs or groups of atoms can bond into a bigger structure called a molecule. Our physical bodies are composed of the elements of the mineral kingdom. All the elements have an indwelling intelligence, or elemental; an en-souling entity that uses the form and experience of that element to evolve. Just as you use your human body to pursue your own evolution, so does the elemental intelligence use its form to evolve. And just as within the human kingdom there are various grades of proficiency or attainment, so there are gradations within the mineral kingdom. None are better or worse; all are simply different.

Similar to humans, the indwelling intelligences within the mineral kingdom go through a learning process. They pass tests, which are really demonstrations of proficiency. They integrate certain things, progress and incarnate into more refined, structured bodies within the mineral kingdom. For example, the en-souling intelligence in a grain of dirt or a bit of rock progresses, incarnates and en-souls into greater levels of refinement and proficiency in its expression of the ideal of mineral-ness. It goes through the various structures within the mineral kingdom, finally evolving into a level of refinement which allows it to en-soul a gemstone or a crystal. *Relatively speaking, gemstones and crystals are the Enlightened Masters within the mineral kingdom.*

You may have experienced working with a crystal, perhaps for many years, and then it disappeared or even vanished in your hand while you were meditating, or broke open and felt dead because the indwelling intelligence had chosen to leave it - partly because of the learning it had integrated through interacting with you.

By interacting with humans, these en-souling intelligences often make big shifts and transit into the next kingdom - in the case of a crystal, the plant kingdom. They will then move through the various levels of refinement in the plant kingdom, from plankton and algae into higher, more complex forms of plants, and ultimately into the greatest ideal of expression of tree-ness. Have you not ever experienced a wise, old, Enlightened Master tree?

Then, those intelligences move from tree-ness into the animal kingdom to begin by en-souling a single-celled organism, and then continuing on through the animal kingdom. The highest expressions - the 'Enlightened Masters'- of the animal kingdom are most often found en-souling domesticated animals such as the horse, dog, cat and elephant. As they move through the process of refinement and ultimately embrace love, interaction and commitment in the animal kingdom, they graduate into the human kingdom. This is the beginning of the long process of integrating human qualities.

The ultimate expression in human form is to live and act out of sacred qualities. These sacred (also known as alchemical) qualities include, yet are not limited to: abundance, adaptability, allowance, acceptance, appreciation, aspiration, attunement, awakening, awareness, belief, calm assurance, charm, clarity of intention, clarity of perception, compassion, connectedness, courage, curiosity, discernment, endurance, faith, flow, purity, gratitude, harmlessness, harmony, honesty, hope, humility, illumination, innocence, inspiration, integrity, intuition, is-ness, joy, kindness, knowing, loyalty, mercy, oneness, openness, patience, realisation, receptivity, revelation, sense of humour, serenity, spiritual intelligence, surrender, timelessness, tolerance, trust, unconditional love, understanding, unity, wisdom and worthiness.

All of these sacred qualities are present deep within the cave of the human heart, our being, where our highest potential resides. Our journey as human beings is to claim these qualities, and then to transform ourselves so that we are the embodiment of these qualities. To do this, we must transform our thoughts, feelings, beliefs and behaviours. Calling forth any particular quality from our heart, surrendering to the experience of *feeling* that particular quality, and allowing it to integrate as part of who we are and how we choose to express, is part of the Cosmosis® Personal Spiritual Alchemical Journey..

Humility is having a correct sense of proportion of where you are at, how far you've come, and how far you have to go. It is one of the most important sacred qualities to integrate. Being humble means simply accepting your attainment and proficiency on all levels, not underestimating or over estimating oneself in any way.

Many people on the spiritual path are full of self importance. They feel that they are better than others because they are 'more spiritual' than them. It is important to remember that there are three hundred and fifty two levels of consciousness between base human consciousness and Creative Source. Someone who has attained to the level of Planetary Realiser is only on level seven, so they still have three hundred and forty five levels to integrate on their return to Source. This puts things into proportion. Most spiritual teachers, even gurus, are only on level four or five. Beware of believing anyone proclaiming they are 'there', fully God-realised, have learnt everything, or are the best or the most advanced….because that shows an obvious lack of humility.

Every time we progress to the next level, we find ourselves again at the beginning of a vast amount more to integrate. On a side note, I am constantly amazed at how many people proudly proclaim that they have outgrown orthodox religiosity…….. and then go on to tell me all about their guru. They are completely devoted to their guru, whom they venerate to some kind of demi-god status, without realising that they are just caught up in an Eastern religion. That's right! The whole guru and ashram thing is just an Eastern *religion.*

For those of you who are still the students of gurus, it is recommended that you stop it. This is no longer the time of great spiritual teachers. It is now rather the time of great spirits. The shift from spiritual devotees giving their power away to self-proclaimed gurus may cause a temporary unemployment situation in India and elsewhere, but don't be alarmed as 'Upstairs' has a retraining and rehabilitation program underway for them, to teach them how to actually be of some use in the process of training Masters.

You must be discerning. Anyone who claims to have been born fully realised, or to now be completely God-realised, is certainly not that simply by virtue of their claim. Masters do not make outrageous claims because those claims encourage dependency. Masters lead by example and allow the living revelation of their lives, and their presence, to speak for itself. Without exception, any true Master will simply allow others to discern their attainment, and without exception a true Master never makes public claims which set them apart from humanity in any way.

Any soul that has reached some level of attainment in the spiritual initiation process, no matter what degree of attainment, has to retrace their steps in each and every subsequent incarnation. There is no recognition of prior learning in the spiritual initiation process. Every time we incarnate, we agree to totally forget our true identity and everything we know. Given the current conditions on our little planet here, of course, this is not so difficult. Every institution in our culture supports this spiritual amnesia, and it becomes easier as the years go on.

Don't give yourself a hard time about having trouble remembering who you really are. What our parents are unable to suppress, the education and medical systems usually make short work of, as this is their specialty.

Once again, I remind you that all spiritual initiates must re-trace their spiritual steps in each and every incarnation. Only once you have completely fallen asleep and become totally dysfunctional may you then proceed to the phase of spiritual awakening in this lifetime. This involves waking up to your true self and forgetting everything you learned up until that point in this life, so that you can remember what you actually knew before you got here.

You must now discard your false identity that you just spent a lifetime creating. After falling asleep profoundly, you must now wake up profoundly. Now is the time to throw off that which has been assimilated so as to be able to remember that which is deeply known. Only then begins the process of active participation in the creating a new human destiny.

Some of you may be indigenous to this planet, and will have been right through the evolutionary process on Earth. Your energy may have first developed sentiency here as a rock, and gone through faulting and folding to assist this sphere to form her planetary body, developing responsiveness. Then you moved through the plant and animal kingdoms, developing emotions and the beginnings of mind, and now are in the kingdom of humanity. If that is the case, then you probably don't look at the stars with wanderlust.

Other energies in human form here have come afterwards either partly or completely evolving through other systems. Some have issued forth from Source as light-workers, and are part of an immune system response when things have somehow gone awry within creation and a new pattern needs to be integrated.

These light-worker immune response humans are here to first embody the local "pathology" of the current humanity, and then to love that pathology unconditionally. In so doing they hold the patterns for a new and different sacred style of functioning. Once here, such ones become part of the evolving lifewave, and the only way out is to ascend out utilising whatever mechanisms of transcension are available within this sphere. If you are such a one, then welcome home.

How you came to be right here, right now, is not important. The only thing that is really important is how you choose to express your energy now.

This progression through the kingdoms continues from the kingdom of humanity into the kingdom of souls, into the spiritual kingdom, into the kingdom of divinity and on and on.

On the Alchemical path, we first develop planetary rapport and then continue towards universal consciousness.

The Cosmosis® Mentoring Centre offers integrated Personal Spiritual Alchemy development programs within a variety of modern contexts, including counselling, business studies, holistic healing, naturopathy, coaching, mentoring and ascension training.

This training reflects the ancient mystery school experience. We provide training, coaching, mentoring, healing and counselling. We have a Psychologist and a Medical Doctor on staff. All of our coaches and mentors are fully qualified and many are multi modality practitioners.

Visit **http://mysteryschool.org.au**
For more information.

Chapter 3
Crystals: Past, Present and Future

~~~

This world of creational evolution can take two paths. One path is pure energy, which is the raw material of the universal plan, full of potential, but having no form. The other path is matter. Matter has structure and it provides the potential for vehicles of consciousness to evolve.

Life on Earth began with bacteria in the oceans, and the ancients believed that humans came into being because bacteria desired a mobile salt-water environment, which would allow them more possibilities to explore the potentials of sentiency. An interesting world perspective indeed…

The many aspects of the planetary body choose different forms as their vehicle of expression for evolution. There are two streams or expressions of the mineral kingdom: One is through the experience of metals, which has a certain matrix and energy system. The other is along the crystal line, which has a different matrix form and includes gems and the many refined forms of earth (sub-species of rock).

Being formed by nuclear fusion in stars, gold is considered a kind of super-advanced enlightened Master of the metal kingdom. Just as one spiritual path is not better than another, metals are no better than crystals and vice versa. They are simply different, the same yet different as a way of expression.

The most uniform, symmetrically structured forms of matter on this planet are crystals. Crystals are composed of cells repeatedly arranged in a very ordered matrix. The internal and external form of a crystal is the same. If you crush up a crystal and then look at the bits, they look essentially the same as the original form of the whole crystal.

The quartz crystal is one of the most beautiful crystal forms. Quartz is a mixture of silicon and oxygen, which are amongst the most abundant chemical elements on the planet.

The knowledge of the uses of quartz crystal is immense and widespread. Charged with electromagnetic energies that they accumulate as they grow within the depths of the Earth over millions of years, crystals chronicle the history of the world and the wisdom of the ages. They are designed to, and love to, absorb energies. They then alter those energies and radiate them.

If you squeeze a gemstone or a crystal, it releases an electric charge[2]. When you release the pressure on the crystal, it regenerates itself. If you squeeze it again, it generates another electric charge. The way it works is that when crystals are oscillated - squeezed and released - they experience pressure fluctuations, so that they vibrate at a particular frequency, and transmit and store energy at a particular frequency. This is how digital watches, computers or any transmitter or receiver on the planet works when it uses crystal technology (anything with a digital oscillator).

Crystals have a remarkable ability to store and amplify energy. Simply look at how every digital watch or computer works. They all run crystal digital oscillators at their hearts to operate their time clock and central processing unit. Every radio and TV station uses a quartz crystal to amplify and transmit. The Quartz is cut and tuned to a particular size, connected up to an amplifying resonator, and then hooked up to the station's aerial to transmit the signal. It has been well known for millennia that crystals have this piezo electric effect.

It is difficult to acquire good quality crystals because many go to the electronics industry. The premium mines in

---

[2] This is known as the piezo electric effect

Australia haven't been releasing crystals onto the market for many years, because overseas interests bought the mining rights for the electronics industry, primarily in Japan. Over the last fifty years or so, the electronics industry in particular have fiercely sought the rights to mine and cut into tiny bits the best quality crystals from around the world. Only masculine (clear) crystals are useful in computers and digital watches. High quality and clarity female (opaque/milky) quartz is mainly found in gold shards. In the strip mining process, these shards get destroyed. It is sad that female crystals are considered pretty useless and are largely destroyed, and therefore tend to be suppressed. They have wonderful properties, functions and abilities and are important in holding and restoring a balance.

In the late sixties, the Japanese developed a micro-fibre memory technology for computers. It is a crystal about two inches long and two inches wide able to store unbelievable amounts of data information at very high speed (measured in terra-quads), and stored as light. To date this technology is only really applied to military applications.

In Atlantis and other civilizations, crystals were used to store enormous amounts of energy and light. In Atlantis, Egypt, Sumeria and other civilisations, crystal technology was used to light cities. Crystal banks would store light during the day, and crystal energy was transmitted wirelessly to crystals mounted all over the city, glowing bright with perpetual energy from the Earth's magnetic field.

Crystal healing was the main form of healing in Atlantis and Egypt. In Egypt, a serious healing session was done with thirteen people. Twelve would hold crystals: one at the head, one at the feet, one holding each hand, one at each shoulder, one with their hands on the heart centre, one at each of the knees. The thirteenth person was the priest or priestess facilitating the session. It was hard to stay in denial of the truth with this kind of focus. Addressing denial re-creates balance, harmony and healing: there is either truth, or denial and avoidance of truth.

Aspects of every kingdom of nature hold a certain responsibility or chosen learning to birth a new age. On the electromagnetic level, the mineral kingdom has a big role to play in this new age of Aquarius. It is not just as simple as saying that the more negatively polarised or feminine crystals have a role. It is an interaction between feminine and masculine. There certainly is an enormous amount of wisdom stored within the feminine aspects of nature. But without the masculine influence, that wisdom tends not to be expressed, or is expressed in a way that is often self-defeating, going around in circles, or in locked-up patterns. On their own, the masculine forces tend to go off half-cocked. It is very important for the feminine and masculine to work together, and so bring these energies into balance.

Crystals allow us to access a huge range of healing energies. You can send them love and then focus the outflow of energy from the crystal to any disharmony within your physical, emotional, mental or spiritual bodies. The energy outflow from different types of crystals is beneficial to various parts of the body, and crystals may be worn on the body or placed strategically in your home to work their magic.

Crystals allow you to attune to particular spiritual energies in much the same way you tune into a radio station. Once you are tuned in, you can then begin to slowly unlock parts of yourself currently entombed by fear and prejudice, avoidance and denial. As we tune into higher and higher energies, our bodies heal themselves. As you lighten your bodies, you will notice an improvement in general health. This is partly because your new higher vibration is no longer a compatible host carrier for the many viruses in the world today. As your overall attitude towards health improves, you will have more energy. This in turn speeds up the self-healing pattern you have set up in your mind.

Working with crystals improves your intuition, so you begin to be "sure" of what to do in any moment when facing with a decision or an obstacle to overcome. This is what we are reclaiming: relearning to source our own love, our own knowing through the heart, our heart's wisdom, our own empowerment. To source from within ourselves - from the Spirit/God knowing within - rather than looking outside of self for validation, for love, for knowing. Experiencing life and learning from our own reflection of choices and consequences is different to blindly and explicitly only taking advice from outside of self. The heart always knows.

Sometimes others can hold bridges and clearer spaces of love and knowing for you. They inspire growth in you, and bring you insights as to how you may become greater. In their wisdom, they may hold the space for you to also come more into attunement and alignment with your own heart's knowing; therefore empowering you, rather than simply telling you what they believe is wise for you.

Sadly however, most spiritual leaders are charismatic rather than inspirational leaders. In the presence of a charismatic leader, you feel as though the leader can do anything. They encourage you to worship them and serve them. Most gurus are charismatic leaders. Hitler was a charismatic leader. This is disempowering to the followers as it encourages them to doubt themselves, and to believe that they need someone outside of themselves as an intermediary between themselves and Source in order to receive true wisdom.

Orthodox religiosity in all of its expressions is essentially charismatic, and promotes a saviourship model of spirituality (spiritual progression through being 'saved' by something outside of oneself).

On the other hand, inspirational leaders make you feel like *you* can accomplish anything. Winston Churchill was an inspirational leader. Understand the difference! Don't follow a charismatic leader if you truly want to evolve spiritually. Instead, find an inspirational leader and take instruction. The path of personal spiritual alchemy is all about transformation through self-mastery, rather than being saved.

Instead of encouraging you to be dependent so as to be 'saved', a spiritual teacher on the true alchemical path simply holds a space of inspiration for you. He/She encourages you to come closer to your own connected alignment, centre, grounded knowing, and will actually teach you that you can reclaim your innate state of knowing, love, wisdom and empowerment. Teach a person to fish rather than give them a fish. This is the true basis of all healing and ascendant teaching. Working with crystals assists you to come into this state of presence and being. It is also a co-creation, and can be empowering to both you and the crystal intelligence, if you don't give your power away or relate to them selfishly. Sacredness, respect and mutual co-creation in joy is a wonderful basis for such learning together with crystals.

Chapter 4

Sacredness, Respect, Wonder, Potential

~~~

Are you able to love a rock?

From the perspective of a crystal, when you sit in one place, experiencing the results of the Earth's evolution for millions of years and the growth in your ideal of crystal-ness, a special kind of wisdom and understanding comes to be held by the crystal.

Like the ancient tree, rooted for a few hundred years, that senses, experiences, integrates and survives everything that has gone on around it; that tree holds a certain, special wisdom. Crystals are much older than the oldest tree, and are especially effective at absorbing and holding energy and its information. This is part of their responsiveness. They experience everything that occurred holographically and magnetically the whole time they have been alive. They store this. They are a repository of all the wisdom as old as they are. A 16-million-year-old crystal potentially links you to all the mastery of life, in all the kingdoms, over its 16-million-year period.

The effectiveness of working with any other being comes down to the respect that you hold for the intelligence en-souled by that being. Without respect, real cooperation is not possible. To truly respect the mineral kingdom, one has to transcend the mentality or belief that humans are somehow better than a rock, tree, animal or anything. Remember, the greater Kingdom of humanity encompasses all indwelling consciousnesses. It is all just God stuff moving within the evolutionary process of Creation. It is vitally important to respect and love the mineral kingdom, and to love all the kingdoms. To work powerfully with the mineral kingdom, you must develop a love bond of mutual joy, understanding and respect for the roles you both will play.

Crystals love sound. Sound waves are instantaneous fluctuations in air pressure or air vibration. As air vibrates, it subjects crystals to pressure fluctuations so it is in time with the music. To some degree, the crystal is squeezed and released and it starts to release energy and sing. This is why when you have a lot of crystals around and you play music, you will find they start to release, exchange and transmit energy. The type of music you play is important because the crystal will amplify whatever is harmonically captured. If the music is about unrest, subversion, rejection, rebellion or ego, then that is amplified about seven times and radiated into your environment. If on the other hand it is beautiful music, then the crystal will amplify and radiate that as far as its influence allows. Just as with the development of a human, how many subtle bodies they have active and how conscious they are determines the sphere and extent of one's influence; the same goes for a crystal.

How much a crystal has been loved, and how many issues it holds concerning its past, affects its sphere of influence. For example, being ripped out of the ground and not being loved by human beings is an issue for crystals. It traumatises them.

Crystals that have been broken off at their base and have some of the base material present are probably still alive and growing, albeit pretty slowly. If it hasn't got the base, it is the dead body of a crystal. It still has the electronic ability to process energy - so it may be a useful tool - yet the soul intelligence of the crystal is no longer present. A crystal that is still alive is an evolving being-ness, with an inherent intelligence, understanding, and possessing expertise in crystal-ness and transforming energy. Working with it is a co-creation. If it is dead or a tumbled stone, then it is more a tool you use as an extension of your own energy matrix. You may get a response from the knowing from which that crystal is sourced, but not from the crystal itself.

Crystals also don't like being skinned. If they are cut and nicely polished, they are skinned and probably dead. Crystals and gemstones that have been cooked in hot dye are not happy. How pretty a crystal appears has nothing to do with its attainment.

Positive clear crystals (male) are transmitters: they amplify, tonify and stimulate. If you want to concentrate energy, you use a masculine crystal. Masculine crystals, like the masculine polarity in any kingdom, tend to be amplifiers and transmitters. Not useful, of course, without the receptive polarity and without something to transmit, which comes from the feminine. This is also why it is important to balance the masculine and feminine within you.

If a crystal is very clear yet also displays cloudiness, it may be balanced in masculine and feminine energies, and be capable of transmitting or receiving. Crystals that are balanced masculine and feminine are very good for balancing the masculine and feminine within a plant or within a person.

A cloudy or female crystal is a receiver, rather than a transmitter. It is used to temper energies, reduce intensity, to draw out energies, or used to disperse a focused point of energy.

Some crystals might look very nice, but what they imbued during their growth has wrecked them. Send them love, then feel what they emit. Human civilisations have built great cites near vast crystal caverns, because they understood how they could use them to amplify energy for mind control of the populace. Those civilisations may have been involved in all kinds of human sacrifice, suppression, fear and subjugation so common in our history. The crystals that have been deliberately used for thousands of years to perpetuate that kind of ethos - which is very different to the actualisation of the Golden Age we would all like to see on the Earth - are not the kinds of crystals that you would want to work with. You could pick up such a crystal and send love to it, and because it is an evolved being you would get a response. But if that response was sexual attraction to animals, or something as disturbing, I personally would smash the crystal. If it is an amplifier that holds that kind of energy, it will not be able to contribute to the Golden Age and the kind of world we want our children to inherit.

An enormous amount of people are deliberately mining these kinds of crystals. It would be performing a great service, to the Golden Age and for the planet, to lose those crystals; to break them, as they have been corrupted by their interaction with corrupt societies in Earth's past.

I search the world for crystals that have come from places of great clarity and purity. I look to source them from places where the oracles have existed for an enormous amount of time; where people have been devoted to equality, oneness, the ascension process and moving into mutual interdependence within a spiritual context. The crystals that we offer you have been cleansed, programmed and activated to work with you to assist you to come to a greater understanding, with all the kingdoms of nature and within yourself, and to amplify the love you radiate.

The most advanced members of the various kingdoms of nature have to continuously move forward into the next kingdom, so the next lowest kingdom can start to process them in. About 250,000 years ago, the door from the animal kingdom into the kingdom of humanity was effectively closed. Except for very rare exceptions in the last 40,000 years, it remained closed. It is very difficult for advanced animals to move into the human kingdom, because humans were not ascending out and moving into the kingdom of souls. Everything backed up. In 2000 years on this planet, within a system actually designed to produce ascension, there were only forty two ascensions between the time Jesus left and 1968. This is far less than one per generation! No judgment intended, but something radically screwed up with the system. Since the mid 90's, we averaged 5000-8000 ascensions a year, which is much more on track, but still way under what a system like this needs to be producing to meet its agreed goals and levels in evolutionary terms. These ascending souls, who are moving into the ranks of elder sisters and brothers of the race, have a role of stewardship for the planet. Unfortunately, the overwhelming majority of these advancing souls remain embroiled to an alarming degree in glamour, illusion, psychological immaturity and self-aggrandisement. Most of these ascending souls have already fallen, because they simply did not have the correct psychological foundation to support an ascended consciousness.

With the general increase in the levels of spiritual light upon and within our beloved Earth, many long-serving initiates have scraped through into the advanced phases of human actualisation with the bare minimum proficiency and mastery on many levels. Hence, we see so many unintegrated teachers spreading ego/fear-based nonsense to gullible followers. We also have huge numbers of psychic channels, with little or no training in this lifetime, spreading ridiculous nonsense. From my experience, over 98% of channeled information is contaminated by fear and untruths, to such a degree that it is essentially useless. Still, people want to believe in free lunches, so they keep listening. You must learn discernment my friends: if it sounds too good to be true, it probably is. Far better, you learn to listen to the voice of the

Spirit within you and interpret it through your own psyche, which has been adequately trained and prepared to a degree of clarity and purity of heart allowing you to interpret the musings of spirit accurately yourself.

Anyway, that's enough on the masses of psychic weirdness out there for the moment. When you get to about the sixth phase in the human actualisation process, you have a choice to: move out of the physical realm and continue your process in the kingdom of souls, or remain embodied on the planet to help those who are moving into the levels where you are. Many members of humanity who could move onto the next kingdom are now choosing to remain as teachers. You have to be aware of the choices you are beginning to lock in, because if not in this lifetime, in a few lifetimes - provided you remain focused - you could conceivably complete planetary ascension and move on seriously into your cosmic evolution.

The back log of about 160,000 ascension candidates who were close, but didn't make it through in the last age of Pisces, has largely been cleared. As a consequence, new parameters are being set around the ascension process to stem the tide of unintegrated ascending creatures. Now that things are moving again, we are starting to see the more evolved animals beginning to incarnate into the human kingdom.

Thankfully also, the evolutionary system lords are encouraging many of these human creatures who have recently started supporting an ascended consciousness to hang around on Earth, teaching what they most need to learn before moving on.

Now, new candidates are moving through the middle levels of the human actualisation process. If you genuinely sense in your heart that this is what is occurring for you, then you need to be head down, seriously committed to service and giving back, as this is a prerequisite for moving on. You need to set certain things in motion, such as creating the legacy of a unique and loving contribution you want to leave the planet.

Do you want to achieve a certain level in the ascension process, and then leave the planet - not be in a physical body and continue the process on the inner planes? This is a valid choice. However, the planet needs many to stay to teach and heal during this period of accelerated change. With the reprogramming and restructuring for the new paradigm into the Golden Age, and with so many floundering and so many false prophets or unintegrated teachers whose motives are contaminated by fear, I feel we need pure and clear high level ascension candidates as teachers staying in physical bodies, as mums, solicitors, firemen, garbage men, doctors, all walks of life.

Over the last six thousand years, we have put up with the patriarchal playground and an enormous amount of fear-based activities like burning at the stake, being garroted, suppression of the feminine, and generally not teaching people how to access and operate their own innate Godliness. We are over it now. Through the very tough times, we put up with so much invalidation and persecution; we became so scarred as human beings, and yet so evolved as spiritual beings. Now things are actually improving, it might be an interesting choice to hang around for some more pleasant experiences, and to see the fruits of our labour after having been those torch bearers through the dark ages. Within a couple of generations, we will see the planet, life and civilisation, existing as we have dreamed of for so long. Consider renewing your spiritual service contract for another 2000-5000 years, and have a string of lives where you experience the Golden Age. Work on yourselves; confront your fears, avoidances, illusions and denials and release the underlying judgments so your inner wisdom can be awakened.

The vast majority of people in the ascension movement have no idea of their options. Start making some serious decisions about your process as you move into the levels of universal consciousness, as an integrated ascending creature. This is not an ego-based thing, but if you get really good marks for purity of heart, purity of intention and psychological clarity on a world which has been so ignorant, closeted, paranoid and set up as a fear farm, it looks very good on your cosmic resume. You can then put your hand up and say what position you are interested in as you move into higher spheres of evolution. This is where potential universal and cosmic employers will look for extremely promising ascension candidates, who have achieved high levels of clarity and purity from tough schools where it is difficult to get good marks.

There are whole streams of evolution out there where all they do is count things and keep records. If you don't start setting your sights and including in your spiritual goals the sorts of things you want to move into when you leave this planet, you will find yourself sucked into some mundane job for a very long time.

OK, OK, I hear you.... I'd better share a bit more about how 'Upstairs' (the universal evolutionary forces) is changing the parameters of the evolutionary process here. I know many of you, who are following a traditional ascension path, have been wondering why your sadhana (spiritual discipline and service) just isn't producing the results it is supposed to. Well worry no more, as hopefully this book will explain how things are now.

Chapter 5
Streams of Evolution and the Human Actualisation Process

~~~

The 3 Streams of Evolution

All life springs from the same source, the Source of all life. We are one in that perspective, varied expressions of the same Source. We experience many cycles of expression. We develop and evolve through our experiences, how we respond, how we learn and what we learn. This is the process of actualisation or evolution.

There are only three types of expressions for life in the broadest terms. There are three great kingdoms or streams of evolution to be alive within: the Angelic, the Elohim and the Human streams. All living beings are either of Angelic, Elohim or Human expression.

Within each stream, there are ascending levels of development, refinement and mastery. As each aspect of the life of Source expresses and experiences repeatedly within a kingdom, each aspect evolves. We evolve into greater and greater mastery and spheres of actualisation, proficiency, responsibility, involvement, group synthesis, knowing and service. Our ability to function evolves to realise more of our innate potential.

The Elohim stream of evolution – are the architects, designers, maintainers and repairers of various systems. They design and hold the energy focus for the structures, realms, planes and spheres of existence. They design and focus the various laws and parameters for these systems in which life expresses – from the subatomic to the greatest macro-scales and meta-systems of Creation. A universe and all its specific parameters and laws are designed, focused, maintained, repaired, adjusted as required by the Elohim.

Elohim do not have free will as we understand it. However, they are self-determining way beyond our ability to conceive. They design and focus the ideal, and monitor the outplay of life within systems, responding as required to maintain homeostasis (balance and harmony) between mutually inter-dependent systems within Creation. Their purpose comes as directives, kind of like ideas from the Godhead /Creator /Source. They apply their experience and wisdom within that purpose, and set the ideas into motion by emanating designs and patterns, beaming them downwards as essences of understanding and inspiration. Lower levels of

Elohim then conceive the patterns of nature on all its levels. This is why they are called "the Architects of Creation".

Most Elohim are not incarnate. They are called celestial Elohim. High level Elohim may design such things as galaxies and universes, or whole systems of universes. The original designers of a particular system, such as Earth or our galaxy and universe, are called the Ancients. Some Elohim - called corporeal Elohim - may incarnate/embody from time to time within a system, particularly at a time of transition or accelerated change. These beings provide a kind of closed loop feedback system for the celestial Elohim, giving instant real-time feedback during times of change or healing. Such beings in human form are often the Master Engineers; they just understand the workings of the universe in almost an unnatural way. Nikola Tesla was such an embodiment. The being known as St. Germain (Master R) is also such a soul.

The very lowest basic building block expression of the Elohim kingdom, when incarnate, is bacteria. At the lowest level of sentient life, bacteria are the designers and also the powerhouses of Creation.

When system disharmony is sensed by the Elohim, the response, maintenance and repair may occur over vast periods of time, in human terms, within eternity. Remember, eternity is beyond all of time; and Elohim exist through and beyond even eternity itself, beyond time, into pure being. Beyond time is forever, beyond forever is all of time, beyond all of time is eternity. From the perspective of the Elohim, the time taken from the initial sensing of disharmony within some part of a system - say within our galaxy or planet - and their response of organising a solution may be exceedingly fast and efficient, perhaps 2-3 seconds in their experience of the passage of moments from their perspective. Yet this may equate to a subjective 200,000 or so solar orbits of Earth-time in human terms! Time is relative. And in the bigger scheme of things, long periods of time can be mere blinks and blips. The alchemical key to mastery of time is that it 'All just Is'.

Who *builds* the plans? Well, that is the various grades of 'builders', the lower grades and levels of the Elohim stream of evolution.

The Angelic stream of evolution – are the embodiments of *processes of life themselves*. The angels are the motive life, the actual *processes*, which put the plans into action on a systemic level. Angelics are the vivifying processes that the Creative Plan has set parameters and designs for.

In relations to each other, the Elohim and the Angelics form a synergistic pair. In creational terms, the Elohim are relatively yang/active, transmitting energy information; and the Angelics are relatively yin/receptive of transmitted energy information. The Angelics flow into process, in response to the active design transmissions of the Elohim.

This is what angels actually are: embodiments of the different processes within Creation. They are not lovely women with wings. Think of a process, and there is an Angelic being embodying that process. Photosynthesis is a process. It is therefore embodied by an Angelic intelligence; you could say the Angel of photosynthesis. Ascension is a process, fire is a process; there are billions of different processes all en-souled by the many grades and sophistications of Angelics. Elohim design and hold the patterns, Angelics embody the *processes* involved in the ongoing creation, development, repair, growth and existence of Creation. Angelics do not have free will. Their purpose is dictated by the process they embody, and they simply carry that out.

Some processes are more evolved and complex than others. One could classify various processes - if you had to - from the most basic and simple, to hugely over-arching systems that encompass many, many levels of other processes grouped within them; and there is a range of Angelics to match each level. On Earth, for example, a rich ecosystem such as the entirety of an ocean, mountain range with all its life forms, rainforests, and all aspects of the land/planet and Creation, have larger systemic sets of processes, with more evolved Angelic beings embodying them than that embodying the growth of one single flower. Such high level Angelics are classified as Guardians, often referred to as 'the Guardians of the land'. There are Guardians of humanity also, and Guardians of Creation. This does not mean they guard your safety, as you might think. They are simply high level Angels responsible for embodying and maintaining the integrity of systems of processes. Within that, there are many smaller groupings of processes, such as the soil dynamics, the water dynamics, the plant species inter-relations, down to individual organisms, each animal, each tree, ant, rock etc.

Then, there are Angelic aspects embodying the vast number of processes *within* each individual creature, such as: the circulation within a plant, its photosynthesis, a creature's liver functions, breathing process, moving of muscles …etc, way down to the cellular and molecular levels, to atomic processes and subatomic behaviour. All embodied by different degrees of Angelics. There are Angelics throughout the human body and in nature, in every process within us and every process we are involved in.

The various scales of these entities en-souling processes are called Guardians, Archangels, Angels, Devas, and Elementals (spirit intelligences of the elements themselves). Some process entities have been given specific names such as sylphs, the Angelics embodying the air, salamanders for fire, gnomes for earth and undines for water.

All of these process entities, and the parameters and laws that define and underpin them are designed, maintained and repaired by the Elohim.

The aspects of the Human stream of evolution embody *within* such life forms.

The Elohim design the plans, the Angels embody the functions, and it is the Human stream that embodies the *creatures* and *creation*s themselves.

One is able to learn to interact and commune with both Angelics and Elohim energies. Doing so is entering into what is termed spiritual co-creator status. Another way to look at it is that we, as human beings, are a symbiotic, mutually inter-dependent meld of all three streams of evolution. We are human in perspective and consciousness, yet also holding the patterns along which we were created, and inhabiting vessels (our various bodies) full of Angelic intelligences, interacting with various processes and patterns in our environment and in other kingdoms. So let us choose to work together in harmony. This is the alchemical key to human wisdom.

The Human stream of evolution – encompasses many more kinds of expression besides *Homo Sapiens*. In its truest sense, the Human stream of evolution involves all life expressions that are conscious meldings of both the plan of Creation, and the outpouring processes of Creation.

The human stream is all about the evolution of ascending consciousness. The form that evolving consciousness takes is irrelevant. The Human stream begins in any system wherein the Elohim and Angelic streams have come together to produce a suitable vehicle for the evolution of human consciousness.

Beings on the Human stream of evolution *embody* the creatures of Creation themselves (which includes beings in light-*bodies*), and have their own particular learning and evolution towards Source-realisation. At certain levels of evolution, Humans claim their free-will status, either late in the animal kingdom or early on as a human being. Their evolution incorporates the use of free will to resist the temptations of the temporal forms of sensibility of time and space, to consciously choose the opening of the heart to live as beings of unconditional love.

The process of Source-realisation involves progressively coming more into agreement with the Will and Truth of All That Is, over staged degrees.

Although many claim to be completely God-realised and 'God's second cousin', it is complete nonsense. Such claims are testimony to unintegrated growth and gaping holes in that person's development. If someone was truly God-realised (Source-realised), they would be immortal and so much more than just a loving soul. They would have great supernatural powers, rather than just a few somewhat extraordinary powers. In these moments, you can count on two hands the truly divinely illumined souls on the planet, and no genuine illuminated being would ever claim publicly to be so.

Those evolving through the Human stream may move into management roles on grander and grander scales. The degree of proficiency one aims for dictates one's actualised abilities and suitability for service. It is never too late to learn. It is never too late to change. Evolution means surrendering to your innate potential, to a new way, and it means *changing*.

So seize the day and always be the best you can be! Seek the training and embody the learning. Seek further integration, and expand into the new of truth, synthesis and service. We all have limitless potential to realise - if we choose - as we journey through eternity. The more one is grateful for the opportunity to live and learn, not taking experiences personally, and the more one integrates mastery and embodies the many sacred qualities, the more we progress towards supporting an ascended consciousness.

Gratitude is the key to manifestation. The stronger the foundations of our development, the more integration we embody in becoming a Source-realised being. Know that you are not your experiences. Marshal yourself whole-heartedly to learn, develop and integrate all the alchemical sacred qualities. Roles and positions throughout Creation are assumed based on merit – on ability, actualisation and demonstrated achievement.

All are equally loved, nurtured and cherished by Source. God/Source *is* inherently loving and benevolent. We are aspects of Source with free will; there is no judgment. There is life, which also brings love and light, and, for humanity, there is free will. We must choose to release the old, embrace and embody the new of our potential, step after step, moment after moment, and between the moments, which is where change happens. This requires *courage*, which brings great *joy*. These two sacred qualities, along with *love* and *wisdom*, are the prime themes of this particular universe, as designed and focused by the Elohim. The way for humanity to ascend through this system invariably involves mustering the courage to follow the truth, to feel the fear and do it anyway, while experiencing joy and embodying love-consciousness.

The Seven Phases of Human Actualisation

Much has been written through the ages on the process of growth and development of human beings. Within the COSMOSIS® Process - for the sake of clarity and consistency - we have the following understanding of the scope and potential of the human development experience, which underpins the entire COSMOSIS® Transformational Process. This understanding aligns with the new parameters of the human self-actualisation process, which have recently been implemented by the evolutionary forces responsible for this sphere.

Everyone undergoes the first three phases of human development to some degree; although very few human individuals ever reach their full potential of physical, emotional and mental development.

Each of these initial three stages last approximately seven years, up to age twenty one.

Stage One - physical development and adaptation. This involves learning to live as a separate unit of human consciousness, detached from the mother (or mother substitute). One must learn to be completely self-sufficient physically to complete this stage. In the first 7 years of life, the physical body essentially grows into a miniature version of the fully grown human. However, the process of weaning oneself from being other-dependent and oriented continues normally way beyond age seven. One must learn to move the body effectively to both transport oneself in space, and also to manipulate material tools for a host of tasks, from feeding to writing. To wholly complete this phase, one must overcome the feeling of separation and disconnection from the safety of the infant support or family, and choose to become self-nourishing and supporting. Most, however, learn how to manipulate others instead, to replace their infant support with selfish fearful co-dependent relationships throughout life, which keep them trapped in fearful self-contraction and the enactment of control dramas.

Stage Two - emotional development and adaptation. This phase is really about socialisation and civilising, and usually commences around age 7 or 8. One becomes aware and interested in the sphere of emotional interaction, and enters a phase of being preoccupied with relating and responding on the emotional level. This leads to awareness as a sexual being also. To achieve the wholeness of emotional maturity, one must learn to nourish oneself emotionally, and that whilst it is foolish to provoke unnecessary emotional reactions, in the final analysis other people's emotional reactions are none of our business. Instead, most people spend a lifetime caught up in cycles of emotional manipulation, such as the guilt-blame-forgiveness dynamic. Many also develop the tendency to act out to manipulate others to make them feel loved, and patterns of punishing those who do not make them feel 'good' emotionally. Children are very sensitive to energetic interactions during this phase. They often become very confused because the words, actions and projections of their significant others are so often conflicting and hypocritical. Lack of emotional wholeness is characterised by dramas, or rejection and rejecting.

Stage Three - mental development and adaptation. Beginning normally in the mid-teens, this phase involves learning to direct the will upon the mental plane, so as to shape one's own universe of perceptions. One learns to use mental projections of thought forms, as well as speech, to manipulate their world. Ideally, one learns to access the world of ideas and concepts. The successful completion of this phase leads to being an even-tempered, intelligent, discerning, independent, respectful, caring, tolerant and loving person. If this phase is stunted, then the resulting adult life is one of acting out to satisfy a feeling of emptiness within. The emptiness is caused by feelings of rejection, being unlovable. This in turn leads to dramas around dysfunctional relationships.

During the first 3 stages of development, everything is sensed to be caused by phenomena within the material world. Those focused wholly within these three stages are known as being 'at effect', as they have not yet realised that the three lower worlds of experience are but effects of higher causes.

Stage Four - Soul awakening - this is begun by the initial undeniable awareness of oneself as a soul journeying through eternity. It marks the beginning of the soul's desire to understand its place within the evolutionary process. It is characterised by the desire towards selfless service to others, and the loss of the need to feel fulfilled solely through the pursuit of bodily and intellectual pleasures. One must be truly devoted to their own growth, yet devoted so as to serve the evolutionary plan. Orthodox religiosity has only ever produced a handful of individuals who have ever progressed past this phase into genuine authentic Divine Source reality. Successfully completing this phase leaves one in the knowing of being but a spot within the macrocosm through which energy is focused. One still identifies with being the point of focus, yet is beginning to know that one is also the energy being focused through that point.

Stage Five - Spiritualisation of the 4-body system (physical, emotional, mental and soul vehicles). Successfully completing this phase leaves one completely devoid of any feelings of separateness. Rather, one knows and feels the human spirit clothed in matter to be undeniably, in all moments, but a small aspect of the much larger beingness which is Source, to the point of feeling united with that Source in every sense. Effectively, one is now completely identified with simultaneously being both a point within the macrocosm though which energy is focused, and indeed that energy also. No separation between the two states of being is known.

Stage Six - Source awakening - the soul clothed in matter becomes aware of its animating spirit, and truly identifies with being one with the Spirit of All Life. One is now simultaneously the point of focus, the energy being focused and the source of that energy. This is the true awakening to supporting an ascended consciousness. Its successful completion also means freedom from the process of ongoing incarnation. This phase requires complete integration of body, mind and spirit in a balanced way.

Stage Seven - the descent of Source reality into the Earth plane. This is the complete merger of the human soul and its Source reality. Consciousness, form, Source and All That Is become one in a symphony of pure awareness. This is divine illumination.

This stage may further be sub-divided into many

phases, and has only ever been actualised completely by a handful of master souls (contrary to so many popular claims):

1. Stepping into true Spiritual Leadership & World Service to effect a bestowal[3]
2. Spiritual Merger: the point where one completes the Planetary Ascension process and officially begins the systematic investigation of their cosmic origins
3. Full and complete Spiritual Activation
4. Becoming a full, equal member, on a Realisation level and operationally, with the inner plane Spiritual Intelligences which guide and oversee the processes of evolution here on Earth
5. Anchoring and activating the universal lightbodies
6. Anchoring and activating the available cosmic lightbodies

---

[3] A bestowal involves introducing something into the evolutionary future of the Earth, in such a way as to create a new potential future, which would not have existed except for your intercession. This new potential must be in alignment with the ideal agreed goals and levels for the planet as expressed by the evolutionary forces responsible for the Earth.

7. Remaining here in service fully embodying Creative Source (the Mother Aspect of Creation) and/or the Mahatma energy (the Father Aspect of Creation)
8. Complete physical ascension and immortality.

Only a few souls in the history of the Earth have ever achieved actualisation beyond phase 5 of the 7th stage. Only a few in any generation even get to phase 2 of the 7th stage. Jesus at the time was only entering the 5th Stage for the first time, and he only entered the higher phases of the 7th stage less than 100 years ago.

I hope this clearly shows you that all these people out there claiming to be God-realised are self-deluded individuals who are legends in their own minds.

This is the age of false prophets, and so many of you have been gullible enough to believe all this nonsense fed to you by self-styled gurus and con artists. You certainly do not find God-realised beings with addictions, or harems, or attachments or fear of any kind.

God/Source Realisation is all about actualisation of the love nature, and that does not necessarily go hand-in-hand with the enlightenment process. God-realised beings are absolutely amazing to experience. Here at the Cosmosis®

Mentoring Centre, we make no claims about being God's second cousin; we simply choose to pass on what we know, and hope that our efforts bring you closer to the realisation of the God/Source within you.

Let's just get real and get on with the job of healing the planet together, instead of basking in the glory of unintegrated glamour and ignorance.

Bear with me; I hope that some of the pieces are starting to fall into place for you.

Hang on, that's right.... We were chatting about working with crystal magic.... So back to that.....

All disharmony is just energy misplaced in the space-time continuum. The way we do that is through our judgments. With judgments, instead of feeling something in the moment, we grab hold of and own that thought, feeling, emotion or idea, and start dragging it along with us. Our judgments drag it out of its place in the space-time continuum, and it creates imbalances. Ultimately that disharmony produces dis-ease.

A big part of healing is assisting someone to release the disharmony, and let it return back to where it is meant to be. Really good healers don't exercise their will at all; they serve as a vessel to allow the energy to return to where it is supposed to be. The energy knows where it is supposed to be. This produces "miracles" in all forms. As humans progress, they hopefully become more selfless, committed to service, release their egoic self-contraction, self-centredness and the illusion that they are the centre of the universe. As that occurs, they become better healers and vessels for teaching, revelation, realisation and inspiration. When you send love to crystals, they mirror and reflect that love back towards you, and into any areas of your energy matrix where there is darkness, ignorance, denial, avoidance or fear. As you send love to them, they will assist you to transcend your fear. Does a crystal resonate with your fear? or does it amplify your actualisation in the ascension process and amplify your love? This is what is important. If you feel a response with a particular crystal that is more love, it may also assist you to see more clearly where your fear is. A loving crystal can make you feel quite uncomfortable. If it amplifies and stimulates stuff within you, which you know is of the lower nature or just generally fear-based, then that crystal is not for you. It doesn't really matter if you don't know why it isn't working with you in a constructive way in the context of ascension. Just because a book says it is supposed to, it doesn't matter. What really matters is the knowing in your own heart.

Chapter 6
Some of My Best Friends Are Crystals

~~~

Be open to what crystal elementals have to say; they will communicate with you. They learn and experiment as they interact with human energy fields. They come to an understanding of how to co-create with you. Become one with the crystal elemental, and it will become a loving extension of you.

How does the crystal cause you to feel? In order to have communication with any other being, you need an affinity and a shared reality so your energies can work together. With both established, communication occurs as the natural order of things.

A stone or crystal can at first seem to have a very potent effect, and then over time that effect can seem to wane. The gift a crystal brings is a transfer of "knowing". The effect can seem to wane because the resonance, the knowing, is held in your field. It doesn't need to produce a continual effect, because the effect has occurred in your field.

You will get to the point where you are sensitive and conscious enough to pick up when a stone is comfortable or not. Like an animal, it will tell you if it is uncomfortable or needs something. You will find them communicating and calling to you. Some crystals crave that interaction.

Once the crystal is aware, know that you are three kingdoms ahead of where it is at: you are a God for that crystal. As far as a crystal is concerned, once you have developed a relationship with it, you are Godlike. It somehow acknowledges you are a more evolved being. It becomes devoted to you, and looks to you for guidance and what lies ahead on its evolutionary path. It wants to serve you, and if it is not able to serve, it is without purpose and feels lost. There is a certain responsibility that comes with this relationship, just like with an animal that you cause to become dependant on you.

As you interact with crystals, you will find that they are linked electromagnetically to the place where they came from. Any crystals that are still growing are also connected to all the other crystals/minerals in the kingdom, on a crystal mass consciousness level. You are developing an enhanced rapport between the kingdom of souls, the kingdom of humanity and the entire mineral kingdom. As you send love to them, you start to cause the great crystal clusters - which effectively form some of the organs, endocrine glands and chakra matrix of the planetary body - to be charged with love. This is one of the reasons that Upstairs (the guiding evolutionary energies of this sphere), over the last 50-60 years, have strongly encouraged us to work with crystals. This is a very important part of increasing the Earth's natural resonant frequency, and assisting her ascension process.

It is important to remember that you cannot solve any problem unless you tackle it from a higher level of consciousness than which it was created by. So, by causing the great subterranean crystal chambers to resonate with unconditional love, we are able to assist in the raising of planetary consciousness generally, which then allows the worlds leaders to look from more 'spiritual' perspectives.

We all have our own Guardian[4]. The planetary body also has a Guardian presence. When we experience a high-level energy somewhere, we really are experiencing the Guardian presence of that point on the planet. It is important to always ask the Guardian's permission if you feel impressed to take some part of the mineral kingdom. It is not important that it looks pretty. It is important if it feels right, and it assists you to attune to that Guardian presence. This is an excellent way to assist you to interact with the mineral kingdom in

---

[4] Guardians are the caretakers, caregivers, creators and de-creators of evolving material forms. They guide the indwelling intelligences of forms towards ever more refined expressions of the divine.

various places on the planet, and assist the planet to move back into a state of harmony.

Crystals are extraordinary mirrors. They receive, they do not retain, in the sense that they do not contribute their own opinion to any energy that moves through them. As you hold a crystal in your left hand, in between the throat and heart charkas, and send love to the crystal, you will get a very clear mirror of your own stuff. It will amplify and send it back through the throat chakra[5], and you will get a very strong intuition for your own issues, denial and avoidance.

As we serve, love and work with a crystal, we are a source of channelling for that crystal. In truth, all activity is about being either a vessel or a channel for energy of some kind. Every crystal that we work with is a channel, just as you are a channel. Crystals work with all sorts of sources that they become aware of. Although they will process just about any kind of energy, even if that energy is self-destructive (much like humans do), being relatively highly evolved within their

---

[5] The Chakras are basically subtle energy centres in the human body. Each chakra externalises within the physical body as one of the main endocrine glands of the body. The soul regulates and controls its material body of form through these glands and the hormones they secrete. They rotate and metabolise energy backwards and forwards between the various planes of existence upon which we live and move and have our being. The magnetic fields generated by these vortices of energy create the aura or human energy field.

own kingdom means they have a preference for more refined energies. It is like they think to themselves "Cool, I sense the love and wisdom and yes, I want to be a source for that. I want some of the love and wisdom to rub off on me and I want to share that."

This is what you can do with a crystal. You choose. "Hey, yes I am in this position, and I want to share this through you for my own benefit, for the benefit of my own kingdom and the benefit of your kingdom and evolution."

If you put a crystal in your left hand and the connection is very strong between your hands and feet, you can connect to the planet and draw energy in: "breathe" energy in through the left-hand chakra, through the heart to potentise it, and then transmit that energy out through the right hand. If the stone is a high-level expression within the mineral kingdom, it embodies a particular sacred quality, character or personality trait of God. You need to experiment yourself and see how you respond to different stones.

Your crystals will become your cherished ascension companions and best friends.

Qualities of Crystals
Amethyst ~~~

Amethyst is clear quartz that has been exposed - while growing - to mild natural cobalt radiation, where certain gases have impregnated within it through geophysical activity within the Earth. The main two elements that contain the colouring are titanium and iron. Amethyst is very useful for soothing and calming, but can also be stimulating. Female Amethyst draws etheric mucous and debris out of the energy field. It is good for activating the crown chakra and bringing the crown and throat into synchronous unison. Amethyst is naturally attuned to the frequency of the Violet Flame, energy of transformation and transmutation. It raises the frequencies of energies in its field, cleansing and clearing fear, and bringing any disharmony into a more harmonious resonance. An Amethyst cave or cluster can hold a presence of the Violet Flame, as well as bring beauty.

Black Obsidian and Black Tourmaline ~~~

Both are incredibly strong at shielding disruptive energies (protection) and grounding. They are good to have near when you are sleeping. Of course, nothing replaces one's free-will choice to have and maintain appropriate boundaries: choosing to only allow in, and radiate from your field, frequencies of the vibration of unconditional love and above. Black Obsidian also holds up an intense mirror of the truth, and can be quite confronting. The truth can be all the issues and feelings that one is denying and avoiding. It can help one to see, feel and know the way to heal. In acknowledging the truth lays the awesome potential to embody love, power and wisdom in balance. Black Tourmaline with terminations is preferable.

Chrysoprase ~~~

I would suggest getting Chrysoprase that is a deep lime green colour, that was mined in Australia, South America or Europe.

Chrysoprase was one of the main stones the Egyptians used to develop seership and stimulate the full activation of the head centres. It brings a mental feeling presence, and a gentle stimulation to the entire head centre. It stimulates and reworks the carotid, the hypothalamus, the anterior and posterior pituitary and pineal glands in the brain, to bring on seership in a big way. When you study, hold some in your left hand, and then when you go to your exam put it in your right hand and send love to it. Lemon Chrysoprase is used to still the mental body.

Citrine ~~~

If amethyst is exposed to cobalt radiation in the earth for long periods of time, it turns into Citrine. Citrine is very mildly radioactive amethyst. Citrine is very stimulating to the mental body. Because it is mildly radioactive, you have to be very careful. Citrine, along with Fluorite, is the main stone you need to work with the mental body for psychological integration.

Fluorite ~~~

When I first started to wear Fluorite a long time ago, it brought up a lot of issues regarding God and Goddess, masculine and feminine. Now, I find I am comfortable with that balance. The melding of energies within Fluorite helps me maintain that balance; particularly when I am around beings, energies, entities and identities that are very unbalanced in the masculine and feminine.

Fluorite, particularly in violets, greens and pinks, is a very powerful balancer for the mental body. It assists you to still the mind, and it is a potent balancer of thinking and feeling. It has a strong influence in the 4-body system in order to bring the masculine and feminine expression into a state of balance. Fluorite comes in masculine and feminine, and with all kinds of inclusions. Inclusions are stuff that got stuck in it while the crystal was growing, and can cause it to behave quite differently.

Haematite ~~~

Haematite is the most amazing and most potent grounding stone that I have ever come across, for anyone who is consciously involved with spiritual work.

Haematite is a form of iron. It has the ability to root you very firmly to your grounding cord and hold you to the planet. If the knowing/energy signature of Haematite is radiated into a room and people are open to receive, they will find themselves much more anchored to the planet, much more connected to their body.

When I radiate Fluorite, it has the effect of increasing mental clarity and being in the moment. It affects the sacral and solar plexus chakras. The solar plexus chakra is the seat of the lower will and lower mind, and the ego operates through it. If I put Haematite and Fluorite together and radiate them, they produce a very grounded, very present mental effect. This starts to connect the mental body with the feeling body.

Jade ~~~

Jade is a very potent stone to stimulate the heart, and it also affects the renal glands. It is not a heart-opener, but it tends to keep the heart open when you have a tendency to contract. Jade, like most of the green stones, will counteract self-contraction, the more powerful depending on the shade. Green stone from New Zealand is the most powerful I have ever found.

Lapis Lazuli ~~~

Heart openness is the natural state of being. I have found that Lapis is probably the most powerful heart stimulator. It works on the throat chakra, and assists the connection between the brow so the intuition works strongly through the heart and throat.

A blocked throat chakra, not having a strong connection between the throat and brow chakra, is probably the biggest barrier to the opening of the heart. Whatever type of vision you experience, direct knowing, or connection to the truth, operates through these two centres. If you get them working together, you find the heart opens. An unwillingness to embrace the truth keeps the heart closed. Self-contraction is fundamentally the denial of truth. The more you are willing to love and accept the truth, the more you will find your heart opens.

Rose Quartz ~~~

Rose quartz is the highest expression of the female form of Quartz, and it holds the vibration of unconditional love. If it has a slight yellowish and violet hue when you hold it up to the sun, it also holds compassion and gratitude. Rose Quartz brings a soft, gentle willingness to love. It encourages you to be open and willing to love beyond where you feel comfortable doing so.

Smoky Quartz ~~~

I wear Smoky when I am working energetically (and Moldavite, which is the remains of a comet that crashed here a long time ago). It took a long time before I needed the intensity of Smoky Quartz. I normally don't encourage people to use Smoky, as it just creates over-stimulation. Most wearing it would find they get an overwork headache feeling in their frontal lobes fairly quickly. If you have any of that very dark artificial stuff, I would hit it with a hammer; destroy it and put it out of its misery[6].

Smoky is naturally brown. Smoky Quartz is clear quartz that has been exposed to mostly cobalt radiation whilst growing. Keep Smoky away from people's heads. If your energy is quite low, you can connect to the planet and sit with a Smoky between your feet and be really energised. You wouldn't want to do this for more than 20 minutes. I wouldn't advise anyone to sleep with Smoky Quartz within 20 feet of them, as it will start to deplete their field like fluorescent lights do. It makes your energy matrix beat and reduces its ability to resist penetration from electromagnetic frequencies, which are like electromagnetic parasites, or airborne elemental parasites and thought forms.

Tiger-Eye ~~~

Deep blue Tiger-Eye holds the signature - the harmonic - of courage, and an amazing sense of tenacity or strength of purpose that

---

[6] The black Smoky Quartz you find in shops has been dumped in a medical reactor for 20 minutes and is highly radioactive, completely dead, and very destructive to the entire chakra system.

I find wonderful. It has a signature of consolidation, and sense of moving in a particular direction.

Tiger-Eye comes in many forms. The basic form is brown. Red Tiger-Eye gives you a sense of general courage in the heart, rather than action. When you hold Tiger-Eye and radiate love to it, it releases and radiates and amplifies a harmonic which is virtually identical to human courage, endurance and perseverance.

Austrian crystals ~~~

These are grown from lead. They have no inherent esoteric value, no en-souling intelligence. However, when they are cut according to very precise Pythagorean geometry, they hold a particular resonance and their interaction with the human energy field can be quite potent.

Chapter 7
Crystal Clear

~~~

How long are you prepared to go without a bath or a shower? Whenever your crystal doesn't feel quite right, or you often find yourself thinking about your crystals, then it is time to cleanse and restore them.

You have to keep your crystals consciously charged with love.

~~~

Crystals love to absorb energy and, over a period of time, get weighed down with low-level energy. This slows down their vibration. When crystals are not clean or full of electromagnetic disharmony, they lose their lustre and don't feel right. They feel really uncomfortable. Female (milky) crystals - being receptive - tend to store energy and get clogged up fairly easily. They need to be cleansed much more often than a masculine crystal.

Crystals love moonlight and many, but not all, love water. Contrary to popular belief, they don't like sunlight. A little bit of sunlight charges them up, but too much gives them sunburn and they get damaged, and lose or change their lustre.

To clear and cleanse your crystals, place them in one litre of warm water with three tablespoons of apple cider vinegar and three tablespoons of sea salt crystals, for 5-10 minutes. If you just want to put them in ordinary water and really infuse it with love, it will not do as good a job as the apple cider vinegar.

An Amethyst cave or cluster (or a big Citrine, or large Smoky Quartz) has a remarkable ability to harmonise any weird energy in crystals. If you have a big cave or cluster, cleanse it once a week or fortnight, then put your crystals on the cluster or in the cave to clear them. The cluster or cave you use will however over time start to change colour.

If you have a lot of crystals, get a large plastic container and put in a cup of apple cider vinegar and several tablespoons of sea salt. Put it in moonlight and you will find they get even more charged up.

NB: Some minerals don't like being in water as they will either dissolve or corrode. Vinegar can react with some minerals. However, most crystal points and clusters will be fine with this method.

Chapter 8
The Circle of Sirius

~~~

"We come together out of a mutual desire to tell you what we wish we had known. When you get to our now, you will know more than we now know. That is part of unconditional love."

The Circle of Sirius is a group-memory consciousness of high-level enlightened beings within many kingdoms. There are aspects of the Guardian energy, which are very pure and clear, which form part of the Circle of Sirius. On this planet, the Guardian energy is the most evolved expression of the Devic or Angelic energy. Highly evolved humans who possess a high level of purity and clarity automatically become part of the Circle energies within their particular sphere. Beings come together to contribute all that they know, without condition, to form this group-memory complex as a trusted source for channelling, from within the form and formless worlds, and from the heartlands that underlie and are beyond the formless worlds of Creation.

The highest levels of the Circle of Sirius are beings associated with this universe, which are very close to making the transition into what they call complete bliss. They are completely beyond the experience of existence. We are talking beyond pure energy, beyond form, beyond intelligence and beyond all influences as we know and understand them. They are about to completely move out of this evolution of Creation entirely. It is just the next step in their process. They say there is intense pure activity involved in complete bliss, but there will be no form, no force, no existence and no energy. They say the last thing they want to do, before they move onto that experience, is pass everything they know on to you and me, because we are the lowest level they can reach. Our abilities are at the very bottom level that is able to move into this group-memory composite. They hope that if they can pass on everything that they know to any "lower being" that is capable of meeting their standards of clarity and purity, then when that being gets to the level where they are at, the whole system will progress.

I find the beings and intelligences associated with the Circle of Sirius to be astoundingly clear, vibrant, pure of motive, unconditional and possessing all the sacred qualities that we aspire to. Yet, when they commune with me they say, "We are far from perfect, we are very aware of our weaknesses, there is no possible judgment of you because what you are experiencing is contained within our learning."

When asked about their nature; this was their response[7]:

"We refer to ourselves as the Circle of Sirius because each of our 9 energies is equal and separate, but when joined and aligned to the Source of All, creates a more powerful force because of the combined wisdom and knowledge that we bring. If you were to describe our energy, you would see it as a huge swirling mass of the most vibrant colours – so bright and united that it gives out the brightest light and hence the bright white light. We are "located" (your terms) so that we represent and can reach through the parts of your heavens known as Sirius, because the energy vortex there is a little more direct and true than in some places in the heavens. However, we are not really located there, as you would realise and know, because we are part of you and your energy and the combined energy of the planet and its peoples.

---

[7] This channeling used with the kind permission of my dear friend Alan Duff. I was involved in a channeling group with Alan for many years.

We are now at such a stage in our journey that our task is timeless. This is as it is for us. We have journeyed and we are now close to 'home'. Our final task before enlightenment, or complete bliss, is to help your Earth and other worlds to lighten their experience and its energies, so that the light can enter and lift you to levels not previously known. We know it is difficult for you in an earthly form to accept us as an abstract concept; the linear human mind wishes to see us in a concrete form, or with a particular presence. We can 'be' as you choose us to be, for we are ONE with All That 'IS'; for if you can see all that ever is and will be is a part of GOD, then we are that. We can then communicate with all who are able and willing to listen, as we are able to be what they wish us to be, and what they would wish to see. However, we are of great joy that you, our son, have given permission to speak through you in the language of a human to all souls. Know then in our communications that if the heart 'hears' and the feelings respond, then these can make the mind respond, and so open up to the new and perceive truth. Learning of the truth is therefore an emotional experience, for the healing and feeling chakras need to be involved for real learning to occur. So make the message emotional, personal and reflect your joy and knowing – let people see that the spirit can soar without the judging brain.

We are 9 because of the unity of that number. Three times the triad, and three times a trio of energy sources from the various Sources that constitute life. The first triad is a melding of the life streams of the dual creative aspects of the 'Heartlanders'[8]: those beings from other galaxies within your local universe who have spiritually attained, plus the life essence of other outer universes. The second triad melds the essences of the dimensions which are invisible on the concrete form of existence; and the third triad melds the hierarchies of those who have evolved through mortal creature upliftment.

Our three from the heartlands and outer universes bring such knowledge and wisdom on places not yet reached by others, in terms of technology and adaption to environments. We know of thought transference and even spiritual transference, for we have recently experienced these learnings. We can understand true and dissolute spirituality, and are able to see what many have yet to learn from their experiences. We provide inspiration as to the way to bliss, and are able to demonstrate and teach spirituality away from the grounded trappings of other existences.

---

[8] The Heartlanders are the beings who exist within the creative heart (sometimes termed the void) of a system of creation. Their lives are neither formless or timeless because they pre-exist both time and space

The second of the triads have lived in such dimensions that we understand as formless life. We have not needed to exist in concrete ways - nor will we ever - and we bring the conglomerate of experiences and knowledge, for we have access to the Divine Consciousness of all knowledge and truths from all worlds. We have been personified under many names including wandjinas, spirit people, elves, faeries, spirit guides, doorkeepers, guardian spirits, spirits of the land, archangels and many more.

Our third group have lived Earthly concrete lives, and we have collectively experienced all that is "human". We have been the masters, teachers, mystics, wizards, composers, artists, musicians, authors, indeed all occupations; and for the most part, our lives have been lived simply without recognition of any kind. We contribute all we have learnt on our journey to date. We are the translators of the Circle, bringing the knowing through the many lenses available to us from our lives upon many, many planets in the universes. For the truth lives and is alive and is part of all you are. And so the Circle of Sirius is the way to the 'IS'. We can be in any "form", but are always and in all ways, glowing, unique, humble, grateful, but with a mission to support, help, love, care, reduce fear and bring you "home".

As many of us have lived earthly lives since time began, we may talk of "great" events in your history from the perspective of those who were there. We have lived lives beyond any group who have lived and do live on your planet. We have also "lived" on countless other planets in different galaxies and in different dimensions. So we have been blessed with those experiences and knowledge that your brain may find difficult to grasp, in the same way that it finds infinity or space difficult to grasp – endless, beginning-less but eternal. And for this work we call ourselves the Circle of Sirius, because we wish to make the point that we are a group spirit, rather than a single entity. And of our mission, and from our reflected knowledge, we see that your original relationship with the land and with All That Is - which was based upon a natural affinity and identity of love and divine and natural law - has been polluted by fear into a different kind of ownership concept. We know no judgment here; it simply is, and we simply choose to restore the balance. With the association with others of our outer Circle - such as you our beloved son - who balance their experiences with ours, so then may we bring truth, wisdom and love to all we influence.

For we have loved

In all possible forms

And of every possible thing, being or event.

And have lived our love

And have drawn love

From every source.

To be what we are

And to bring what we know

To all that live

Have lived

And will live.

To eternity and bliss,

May LOVE Restore the Balance………..

Rest in our LOVE,   the Circle of Sirius

Chapter 9

Attunement Meditation

~~~

This attunement is through the heart of the planet - planetary heart - to the vast crystal intelligence and repository of wisdom concerning the processes of physical evolution on our Earth.

Hold a crystal that you feel is most appropriate for this attunement in your left hand, between your heart and throat chakras. Have the crystal pointing towards your throat chakra. If you have it pointing in some other direction, it will be difficult to receive. Send love to your crystal; it will amplify and return that love to you. You don't have to look at it to love it. Emanate your love. Remember, love is a measurable force. With your love you evoke, gently encourage, the intelligence of the crystal to become aware of what is going on outside of itself.

"I love you, I appreciate you and I am grateful for this opportunity to work with you. Please don't put me on a pedestal, because I am only a couple of steps ahead of you."

This communication sets the field for respectful, loving, sacred, humble co-creation as conduits of love.

The crystal will become aware of something outside of itself, and you will get a response. It might have an "ah-ha" experience just like you do when you experience something outside your normal sphere of consciousness.

Now visualise upon the canvas of the mind: feel and know yourself to be inside and outside the crystal. Send love from your heart chakra, and light from your brow chakra, to the crystal. Look down and send love and light to the crystal; at the same time being inside the crystal receiving that love and light. Feel it. You are inside the crystal and outside the crystal, so you are the source to that crystal, and also the receiving aspect.

We invoke the crystalline intelligence within our own energy system to be one with the crystalline structure of the crystal that we are loving.

Now, find yourself within a great crystalline chamber flooded with various hues of the most vibrant colours.

Find yourself bathing in a pool of beautiful turquoise energy, and invite the elemental intelligence of the crystal to come and bathe with you in that pool of turquoise energy.

Within this pool, call forth the Guardians of the mineral kingdom that have guided the faulting and folding, the shifting of the tectonic plates, and the formation of the planet's body. They guide the evolving elementals of the crystals and minerals, and assisted them to provide the planet's physical vehicle. The Guardians are the caretakers, caregivers, nurturers, creators, de-creators and the destroyers. They bring the knowing of Plan and Purpose to the form world, so that such forms can learn to integrate, know and be more love.

Ask to meld your wisdom with the wisdom of the elemental intelligences of the crystal you hold. As you bathe within this crystalline pool, seek an ever greater rapport with the elemental intelligences which en-soul our own bodies. Our bodies are predominantly water and mineral salts. All those minerals in our body are en-souled by these same elemental intelligences. Let's develop a really loving, mutually uplifting working relationship with all of the elemental intelligences within our own bodies. Love your own body, love the elementals and elements within your own body.

Now, call the spirit which oversees the evolution of all crystalline intelligences throughout this whole universe: its knowing, wisdom and love to be with you, so you may know how to best work with the mineral kingdom and assist the evolutionary purpose - the general ascension process - of all these creations. Find yourself confronted by the presence of this spirit of the mineral kingdom handing you a scroll. You take that scroll in your right hand, and place it in the cave of your heart.

Now feel into the pain that the planet experiences with her own elements and elementals, with the way humanity strips, rapes and pillages her body to provide resources to satisfy temporary sense gratification. Feel how she still continues to love, nurture and support, regardless.

Be aware of how the planetary intelligences view humanity's disrespect and dishonour of the Earth Mother. Seek to bring the wisdom of the elementals into your heart and the heart of humanity, and so too the wisdom of how you may ease this tension and bring harmony. Be open to the knowing. Surrender your little will to receive the truth.

Feel the pain in the planet's body, and comfort, love and nurture her. She provides the elements and elemental intelligences from her own body so you can create your body. Your body is part of her body. This is her sacred gift to you. Choose to honour that sacredness, and honour her by honouring and loving your body - in, of, and for love. Feel the power of love, and allow love to restore the balance.

Now - still sending love to the crystal - swap it to your right hand. Feel an outflow of energy as the wisdom, the knowing we have just invoked, is fed in through your throat chakra. Be receptive to that, breathing it in through the throat chakra, and then feeding to the head and the heart. Just absorb that intuitive knowing. This is best brought in through the throat chakra, being the mediator between the upper sensatorium[9] and the heart centre.

Choose to be receptive and feel the knowing, love and wisdom of the mineral kingdom. Through this connection with this crystal intelligence, feel part of your own consciousness move down your body, out the grounding cord – your Earth connection - and down into the Earth. Feel that consciousness move through the planetary ley system (energy channels of the planet, however they flow through the Earth) into the vast subterranean crystal clusters that function as the endocrine glands[10] of our beloved Earth. Feel consciousness go into the crystal cluster that is the equivalent of the pineal gland or crown chakra, into the crystal cluster that is the equivalent of the hypothalamus and pituitary or brow chakra, into the crystal cluster that is the equivalent of the thyroid gland or throat chakra, and into the heart centre of the planet.

---

[9] The upper sensatorium comes into being once the throat, brow and crown chakras alchemically meld into one synthesised sensory centre.
[10] Endocrine glands secrete hormones – information carriers – that regulate systems of an organism, and how the systems interact. Endocrine glands are the master regulators and sustainers, and the physical expression of the major chakras - energy transducers or portals. They are the stepped-down representative of higher dimensional energy expressed in the physical realm.

Now merge with the knowing associated with those vast crystal structures within the planet, and allow your awareness to flow through the ley system into the equivalent of the lower chakras of the planet: the (solar plexus chakra) pancreas, (sacral chakra) gonads and (base chakra) adrenals.

Feel that awareness melding so there is an understanding and a willingness of all these aspects of the planetary body to operate in harmony and love. Feel that harmony of love, truth and peace radiate now throughout the mineral, plant and animal kingdoms, and throughout humanity, the kingdom of souls and spirits in matter. Feel yourself grounded here right now.

This is planetary service: using your energy to uplift and enlighten all the kingdoms of our beloved Earth. Feel that wisdom returning up through the grounding cord. Only be open to anything that is unconditional love and above. If it is not about unconditional love and above and the ongoing enhancement of your soul and spirit and of planetary purpose, if it is not about uplifting your individual enhancement and sovereignty, then it is not what you are about; and you should not choose to receive it. If it is about unconditional love and above, you receive that and bring it into your knowing as a human being, and into the knowing of humanity.

Feel and know that connection on behalf of humanity, and choose on behalf of humanity to operate in harmony with the forces of nature. Feel the strength of these forces of nature. In, of and for love, in service to All That Is, co-create with these energies in love, wisdom and alignment with God's plan.

Know that any time you choose, you can consciously connect to this sacred knowing of nature. It is not up to you to heal anyone; no one made you the 'messiah'. Use your energy in conjunction with the forces of Creation to assist another to return to harmony, and let the spirit of harmony itself decide what that means. Be a vessel. Set up this attunement and alignment, go into conduit, hold this as a space for the client, then surrender to the flow. You don't consciously heal anyone, or exercise your personal will or power. You are the sacred vessel for healing forces and energies to create within the canvas of the reality you are a part of. You are a sacred vessel for healing forces.

"I am a sacred vessel for healing forces that fill me and overflow from me. Healing flows through me to assist others become the perfect harmony for their learning and knowing, so that they may fulfil their part within the plan of Creation"

Hold a conscious intent to be a vessel for loving healing forces. It is not about you healing anyone. People heal themselves. No one can heal another. You can use your energy and ability to hold an attuned space to create a set of environing conditions conducive to healing, which provides the opportunity for people to heal themselves, in co-creation with the flow of healing energies. You can love, nurture and challenge their denial and avoidance in such a way that they are able to return to harmony. Teach them how to fish, don't give them a fish and walk away.

Feel and know your healing potential within. Feel and know yourself as a sacred crystalline chalice containing healing forces, and see that chalice full and overflowing. You are a sacred chalice, a vessel of healing forces that is full to overflowing. You never give to another that which is contained *within* the chalice. You nurture yourself so that you may nurture others. Give of that which *overflows* from the chalice, so that the chalice that you are continues to overflow with healing forces. The healing forces, which overflow, are used to assist another to return to harmony.

Suggested preparatory invocation for healing

~~~

"*Mother/Father God, make me the instrument of Thy peace.*

Mother/Father God, I am a spot within the macrocosm through which energy is focused, and indeed I am that energy.

I now call forth all the healing forces and energies that seek to co-create with me in, of and for love, in service to All That Is.

Only energy vibrations of unconditional love and above may flow through me and to me.

I choose, I know and I feel this and I accept only this.

I am love. I choose love, wisdom and alignment with Plan and Purpose.

I feel and know this.
I am grateful for this opportunity. Thank you."

~~~

Chapter 10
Alchemical Healing Fundamentals

~~~

Your spiritual attainment will dictate the kind of energies you are plugged into. If you are not in a sacred and connected space then, honestly, the healing you do is just an exercise in spiritual masturbation. At the very least, you have to get into this sense of sacredness; feeling how small you are within the grand scheme of things, yet feeling how important your role is as a conduit, connector and channel of energy. Only then will you have a real sense of sacredness and potency.

Ask people who come for healing if they are prepared to accept responsibility for their own reality, as the creator of their own perceptions. Ask if it is their desire to embrace the truth of all that they are. If they say no, the session is a waste of time. You may make money, but you will just pump up flat tyres and that is not serving anyone. They will go flat again, as no real change has been effected. They need to choose to progress, and own their empowerment. When you pump them up to feel good temporarily, you are merely entering a dependent relationship with them. This is not healing.

Empowerment is when truth is reclaimed and lived. As a healer, our responsibility is to 'Know Thyself' and assist others to then 'Know Themselves.'

If you are going to work with someone in a healing context, you need trust, affinity and some shared reality. If the person has no belief in some kind of higher power outside of themselves, don't waste your time or energy. Hold the vision of them being grounded, actualised and integrated. Hold reverence, devotion, sacredness, sincerity and playfulness at the same time. Don't get too serious, or you start to block the energy flow.

To start, I like to connect with the person and genuinely feel love and nurture for them. Sometimes I hug them to begin however always remember that doing a healing session is not an excuse to touch someone where you would normally not touch them. Sadly sexual misconduct amongst healers, especially in the new age movement is rampant. There is never any excuse for a healer or teacher having sex with a client or student.... *NEVER!*

It is also important to remember that you can't be in a space where you need to feed or placate the clients ego. For genuine healing to occur, you have to share with them not what their ego wants to hear, but instead be willing to love them unconditionally and convey the truth to them in a way that promotes growth and insight. All healing comes down to ending the clients denial of their innate potential for harmony and balance within themselves.

To assist the client to move into a greater state of balance and harmony, you have to experience love, balance and harmony within yourself, and hold that as a space for the client during the session. Ensure you have the energy centres of all your bodies (physical, emotional, mental and soul) lined up with each other over the heart centre area. Anchor and ground into the Earth and connect to Source. Align and attune to all the healing forces within Creation. Set up protection, and understand unconditional love is all you are about, and all you will accept. Choose that for yourself and your client.

They need to feel safe, secure, confident, loved, nurtured and supported to be open and receptive. Call in and work with all the guides you are working with in co-creation. Feel the energies working with and through you.

Before you commence any healing, stand behind the person to allow them to feel they are safe. Place your hands on their shoulders and really connect with them, sending genuine love, nurture and support through your hands. Always remember it is about healing more than feeling. Move into a space of witnessing their reality, so they feel you honour their reality. We are not making someone feel good about their dysfunctions; they are here to experience a healing. They know they have stuff. We have to unconditionally accept their present state without judgment. It just is as it is: this is their present state and it is real for them, no matter how absurd or irrational it may feel for you. All denial is irrational, foolish, selfish and cowardly.

You have to really feel where the person is at, and this is why psychological clarity is really important. For example, if the person is feeling really sad and you are in denial of sadness, then your own sadness gets triggered. As soon as you are triggered, you can't help the person; your disharmony and their disharmony get mingled and tangled until it turns into a great mess of disharmony. You have to keep your own disharmony out of it and stay in a place where you just honour, love, nurture and support; this allows them to transmute their disharmony, if they but choose and allow.

You must be able to hold a sense of sacredness for where another person is, and what their chosen learning and current states are. Your grounding cord must be really strong, and you just feel and know that your interaction with this person will create more harmony, balance and awareness. It is not enough to simply intend, you must also remain in self mastery for the magic to work.

It may help to ask the person what they would like to receive from the healing session. Encourage them to not only mention what they would like to transform or heal, but also what they would like to choose and become more of. Emphasise the hope that can be instilled by focusing on choosing from their heart. It is not about you imposing your will, "Oh yes, you are exhibiting these symptoms and feeling like this, therefore you need to leave this room feeling like this." That is just arrogance. You are a vessel, an instrument. Hold a knowing of their soul and spiritual purpose and what makes their heart sing becoming more actualised here and now; and allow that which is for the highest good.

Feel that sacred connection to the universal energy field, and to the Earth's energy matrix. You can cross your hands over your heart with your thumbs crossed, and you will start to feel warmth or energy move between the palms of your hands. Place the person you are working with into conduit with universal energy and with planet Earth. You are channelling harmony with the intention of that person coming into a greater knowing of who they are. All you hold as a vision is less denial, less avoidance, more wisdom, more love. Know that this person is source personified, therefore worthy and loveable.

Genuine Healing

All real healing or transformation comes down to releasing the judgment that is trapping the natural energy flows. Healing only occurs when someone acknowledges creating the state of disharmony they are experiencing, then releases that judgment and embraces the previously judged and rejected feelings, and then releases the feelings/energy which has been displaced by that judgment back to its 'home' within the space/time continuum. It is not necessary to delve into the circumstances of the judgment; it is simply necessary to feel without judgment what 'should' have been felt in the moment the disharmony first began.

The energy, once released, knows where it needs to be. So, all that is really required is to surrender the control that is causing the energy to be displaced in the first place. People are often attached to their current disharmony: they defend misconceptions and dysfunctional energetic connections, rather than face the fear associated with changing. The first responsibility of a healer is to instil hope and courage.

Pain is resistance to change. And if easing pain allows one to 'forget' the root cause of that pain for a time - rather than to acknowledge it, take responsibility for it and restore balance to the energy mess they have made - then it only serves the ego. If, however, easing pain facilitates genuine transformation, then it serves spirit. Spirit is not interested in whether the body/mind is experiencing pain, as pain is the great educator. Spirit simply seeks to make choices, experience the consequences of those choices, and so learn and then re-choose. Spirit is motivated by the desire to learn through the medium of selfless service to all that is. Remember that you are part of all that is and that unconditional love is loving the self yet being selfless.

If a healing modality cleverly relieves pain so that people just go back to doing what caused the pain in the first place, then it is self-indulgent, disempowering, and no real learning will be integrated. It is not about the body/mind; it is about eternal growth and integration.

If someone is really stuck in their disharmony, healing techniques may help. If they are stuck because they are complaining of being a victim and you simply relieve their symptoms, then that cannot possibly help. Taking responsibility for one's current state of disharmony is always necessary for genuine healing. If, however, they just don't have the energy left to approach the process of change, then any technique which frees up energy for that process of change serves spirit. If a technique makes someone better able to acknowledge how they really feel, then spirit is served. Feelings are the eyes of the heart.

Always remember that nothing is real unless we feel it. Unless we truly take responsibility and honestly embrace how we feel, only symptoms may be relieved. In order for the real cause of the disharmony to be eliminated, we must restore harmony within our energy matrix by returning the misplaced energy to its original 'home'.

Techniques based solely upon what people *think* serve only the ego, as the conscious mind is the product of just this incarnation. Consulting the conscious mind about anything will only give you what has been learnt in this life, and nothing more. The mind is not the answer to genuine healing.

We must engage the eternal self. We must open all the channels for energy to flow within ourselves to restore harmony. The fundamental shift towards both mastering our health and the human actualisation process is to stop trying to work it all out by thinking. True understanding has nothing to do with the mind; understanding occurs when the heart knows and illuminates the mind. Believing that one can think themselves back to health and wholeness is the height of intellectual pride, and is putting the cart before the horse.

To work towards the achievement of genuine healing, we must clear and transcend procrastination (fear of success), unworthiness (lack of self-worth), and poor time management (the love of being bored). Only a serious process of transformation can produce long-term change. Incorrect thought patterns, emotional charge ...etc, are really symptoms of displaced energy rather than causes - because nothing in the lower worlds (physical, emotional and mental) is a first cause. Everything below soul level is a symptom. Any technique that clears the soul of the illusions and glamours it creates for itself - so that it may acknowledge the truth of its condition - is wondrous. However, this acknowledgment is just the first step towards transformation.

At the Cosmosis® Mentoring Centre, we teach and facilitate COSMOSIS®: a transformational process in which internal dialoguing and energetic clearing techniques have pivotal roles. These processes work together to release displaced energy by systematically addressing the core issue surrounding our control dramas. This produces genuine psychological insight. Unless genuine psychological insight is achieved, then the same energy state will re-install - albeit in a different guise - as there is not necessarily change in behaviour, thought patterns or feeling orientation. COSMOSIS® massively clears the way for psychological insight. It systematically facilitates the required energetic shifts for genuine transformation by addressing:

1. The installation of new awareness: a new knowing which makes the idea itself of continuing with the previous behaviour completely out of the question.

2. Re-orientation of attitudes, and consequently the viewpoints and applied lenses of perception, resulting in awareness of the old re-asserting, and consequently preventing the reinstallation of old patterning.

3. The awakening of a newfound motivation, which overcomes the inertia of the old patterning.

4. A release of the energetic investment in maintaining attachments that reinforce and contribute to the self-delusion associated with the chosen thought, emotion and feeling activity which produced the self-contraction in the first place.

5. An absence of all habitual survival-based responses and reactions surrounding the entire incident cluster of the issue.

6. Retrieval of memory elements, which were unable to be retrieved due to fragmentation of the memory embers as a result of the pain perception aspects of the issue.

We also offer training courses in Seership[11] and Crystal healing.

More information at http://mysteryschool.org.au

---

[11] Seership is the ancient art of translating higher knowing into understanding on the part of humans within the earthly realm

Chapter 11
Chakra Balancing

~~~

In this simple process - taking approximately 10 minutes - the chakra activity between the physical and etheric[12] bodies is balanced, and the interface between the physical, etheric and emotional bodies is cleared and harmonised. Ultimately, the individual, within themselves, must learn to maintain this balance. You would perform a chakra balancing for someone at most once a week. This will give them a sense of how they can be balanced, and a sense of how they throw themselves off balance. Over time, with tools, they can maintain their own harmony and balance.

The front of the chakras relate to the feeling side of experience, the actual experience of living and being in Creation; and the rear of the chakras relates more to the will to experience.

---

[12] The Etheric body is the electromagnetic blueprint around which the physical cells grow. Kind of like a trellis that you may grow bean plants on.

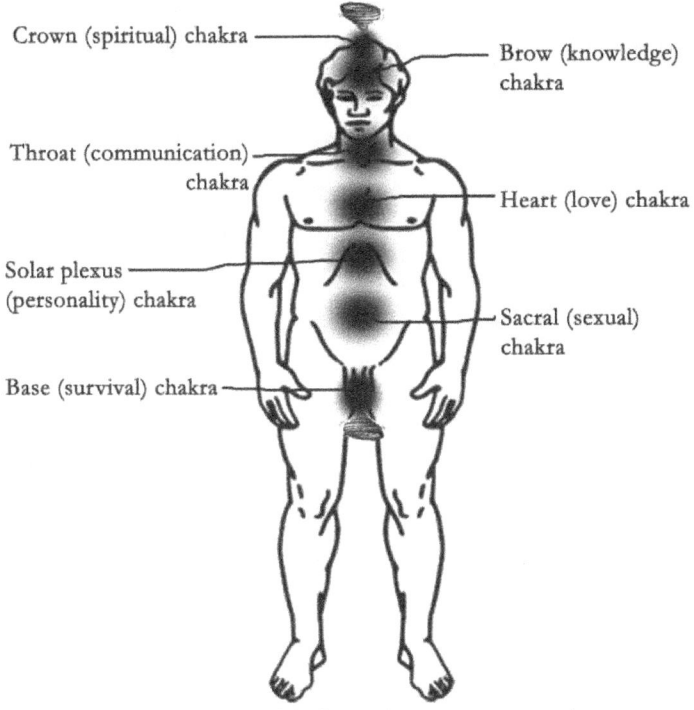

Human Chakras (energy centres)

For most people, the etheric (energy field) body extends out about four centimetres from the physical body. If you allow yourself to be receptive, you will get a tangible sense of where the interface between the various bodies is operating in the chakras.

During the healing session, if you are clairsentient (have a clear sense of feeling), you can close your eyes and feel into your heart space to see the energy. It you are clairvoyant (have a clear sense of seeing), allow your eyes to go slightly out of focus - slightly glazed - and stare about ¼ inch in front of the palm of your left hand, as used in the balancing, to "see" energy patterns. You might need to look at that spot and then close your eyes. You will get intuitive knowing of what you need to do, and what is occurring as visions or symbols. If you are clairaudient (have a clear sense of inner hearing), you might hear specific directions (this is your subconscious mind translating your intuition into words).

As you start crystal healings, you will get a clear *knowing* to assist you to hold states, qualities and energies, and to know what to do to help a person release what their issues are really about. You will get clear guidance if there is something you need to share with the person, or something you need to express in silent communion. As always, be open to inspiration and knowing, as you are co-creating with energy beings.

There is a lot of filtering and judgment around emotion, so it is important to not move into judgment around emotion. Just love emotion and feeling, whatever the experience. When you feel judgment start to shift, you often find you will go back over the area where you have been working, and your hand will start to move further out from their physical body to the various levels. All the time, love and accept the client, no matter what you feel or sense. Don't take what they experience personally; it is their stuff and it is valid, and it is their reality. It is important you don't invalidate their process by starting to judge yourself, their feelings, their issues or them.

You will feel heat and cold in your hands as you move them around the person's field. Cold is balanced: electromagnetic fields are cool to the touch. The blocks, or friction, are where it feels hotter. Stay where it is hot until it feels cool. As you move your hands in and out, you will feel something physical-like, tangible, where there are blockages. If you feel resistance to a certain quality of mastery, a sacred quality, then really feel, amplify and embody that quality yourself. For example, if they are resistant to feeling oneness, then really feel one with the person, and all Creation; and this helps to shift the judgment that underlies their resistance.

To perform a chakra balancing, it is best to stand at the person's side. So, have a stool for them to sit on that is a comfortable height for you, i.e. not too high.

Before you begin, prepare the space, yourself, and the person receiving the balancing. Re-affirm your strong connection to the Earth through your grounding cord. Re-affirm your alignment to Source by visualising and feeling a column of light, extending from above your crown down into the Earth. Re-affirm your attunement by only being open to energies of unconditional love and above. To create a safe and protected space to work, see and feel a golden dome of protection around you and the client.

To begin, place your left hand above the top of their head - their crown - and your right hand behind the rear of their brow chakra. Start by working fairly close, and then feel how far out you need to go. You will find your left hand - above the top of their head - start to move and go to where the main interface is between the emotional and mental bodies of their chakra field (if this is quite a way out, it reflects the person has an amount of detachment from emotion and feeling). Find where there is no harmony, where there is tension, denial and where the energy is blocked. Feel how long you need to stay in one place.

Chakra balancing

Whenever you feel there is no resistance, or you are not feeling anything, it is time to move to their next chakra. As long as you stay in the willingness to serve, the energies will just perform their magic through you. Your right hand will often shake during the process.

Next, move your right hand to the rear of their throat chakra, leaving the left hand stabilised above their crown. Then move to the high heart in the centre of the chest, midway between their heart and throat chakras. This is where the thymus gland is, and is the bridge between the higher and lower chakra energy centres in the body.

Next, move your right hand down to their heart chakra. When you feel it is appropriate, go down to their solar plexus chakra, and then to their sacral chakra. To work on their base chakra, go to the back of the base of their spine. Alternatively, you can go underneath the stool or chair, but you need to have your right hand directly underneath the chakra. You should feel a strong connection to the planet here, as this chakra extends into the Earth. If not, you need to help the person ground. Placing a Haematite on the floor, directly under their base chakra, will assist; or place crystals in between their feet. You can also place your hand crystals in their hands, which will get the energy to flow down.

Once you feel them grounded, reverse your hand positions, and place your right hand above the top of their head. Use your left hand to start at their base chakra, and work up their spine. Feel all their chakras working together in harmony. Your left hand will slowly move up their chakra column. You may feel the need to return to a particular chakra. Your hand will get heavy, and not move, when the energy wants to work in a particular area.

Finally, stand just behind the person and feel around their head. You will either get a sense the chakra balancing is complete, or that there is something else to do.

During a chakra balancing, some people don't feel anything. Some sit and squirm, some move, others swallow or yawn, and when you ask them if they feel anything, they may say no. This is because they are not aware of what was going on. No matter what they express, a balancing effect will have been created in their chakra system.

Chapter 12
Crystal Toolkit and Healing with Crystals

~~~

In your basic toolkit, you want crystals that will recognise you and resonate with you very strongly.

~~~

You can do most things with good quality quartz crystals. It is fantastic if you feel drawn to many different rocks; however, a small amount of stones work. You don't need 500 crystals for crystal healing. A clear masculine quartz wand, a female quartz wand, a citrine wand, matching hand crystals and a few stones is sufficient. Use your intuition when selecting a crystal, the crystal will decide if it likes and resonates with you. It will make itself known to you. Always remember the key to working with crystals—or anything— is to love them. Crystals respond to love, and send it back to you amplified.

~~~

Anything that encourages you to be more comfortable with the truth, and living the consequences of knowing that truth, will open your heart and is valuable. You don't need to cultivate heart-openness. You must cultivate certain expressions of love, certain sacred qualities. However, if you don't enter into denial, and actually embrace and love the truth, you will find that chakras and bodies are activated, stimulated and integrated through a natural unfolding. Provided you are not in denial, a seven-year cycle is the natural order of chakras opening, and the bodies maturing and coming online, when you seriously engage with the alchemical transformational process. Through commitment, discipline, introspection and really choosing to attune yourself to the Universal Consciousness, you are able to accelerate this process.

Prepare yourself as described in the chapter on the preparation for a chakra balancing. When you get into the right space, there is a knowing, an effortless flow, of what needs to occur. You don't think about what you are going to do. You just know, and there is an absence of any sense of control. You are in co-creation, knowing and flow, holding a space. You just become a healing instrument. The energies are working through you and you are grateful for the opportunity to simply be involved. There just needs to be a willingness to play your part as a vessel, and to be a clear and pure transmitter and receiver.

Have the person receiving the healing lie comfortably on the healing table. Have a very masculine crystal (clear) on the table above their head, and a very feminine crystal (cloudy) on the table between their feet. You will feel if the crystals are balanced and comfortable to work together.

Ideally, have a large Rose Quartz or Amethyst underneath the healing table. You may want to put several different crystals under the table - that will come from an intuitive knowing. Feel into the person you will be working with, and you will get a clear sense of this.

Project your intention to perform the healing towards the crystals a little in advance, when you are going to do the healing. The first few times you use the crystals, it will take longer. Love the crystals and introduce them to each other. Thank them and tell them you are very grateful for working together with them. Instruct and program them; tell them what you need them to do. You are God to them; they are aware of you and are willing to serve. Don't let anyone else touch the crystals and put another idea or thought form into them, or surrounding them. Only use them for one purpose. Hold them to your heart centre and love them; they will do what you want them to do, as they become programmed.

Always remain in humility: with a correct sense of perspective, of mutual sacredness, and of how far you have all come, as well as how far you have yet to journey.

Commune with and program the masculine crystal: "I want you to connect with all the crystalline clusters within the Earth, and then move energy around and create a hysteresis loop." The crystal will go, "What the?" It doesn't understand English or words, it understands feeling and impressions. So you have to *feel* for it what you want it to do. Feel the crystal connected into the Earth's magnetic field and the universal field. Feel, know, see and believe that it is connected. You will get a clear intuitive feeling when that connection has been established. The crystal has a kind of 'ah ha' experience and goes "Ok cool. I will do that, no problem." You feel that connection, and you feel the crystal as an agent of energy transmission to create harmony.

Commune with and program the feminine crystal. Follow the same process: "I love you very much and I feel you connected to the universal energy field, to the planet and its crystalline clusters, and to the masculine crystal that is transmitting. I feel you receiving and sending it back into the universal energy field and planet, and cycling around and around like an infinity symbol." You will start to feel that energy beginning to flow. You can move that energy back and forth and around with your hands above the client's body, and it will build. You will feel a huge magnetic field happening.

For hand crystals, ideally select small, very similar female and male quartz crystals, small enough to fit in closed hands. Love them and keep them as a pair, only to be used as hand crystals for healing.

Place the female point up in the left hand, facing the wrist and elbow, and the male crystal point down in the right hand, facing the finger tips (aligned with your body, not your hand). Then the energy can cycle around between these two crystals. The crystal in the left hand has the energy coming up through the body on the left. The energy flow cycles down the other side (right hand side), aided by the right masculine hand crystal pointing down.

The hand crystals run this energy cycle, balancing feminine and masculine, and left and right hemispheres of the brain. We also need to explain to the crystals what they need to do. Go through the process of loving them and feeling a response from them: "Oh yes, what do you want me to do?" Then communicate with them "I need you to work with each other" and then feel this energy moving, up and down, left and right and around and around. It starts to cycle and run both ways. Once the energy is moving one way, you can start to spin it in both directions. Feel and know that to be the case, and you will get this amazing cocoon of energy flowing.

If your hand wands are too big, you lose sensitivity. Most people tend to get a clear wand to transmit healing energies through their body and out through the wand. However, I suggest you get one with masculine and feminine qualities - clear and opaque - so you can use it for not only stimulating someone's field or your own, but also for calming, soothing and drawing stagnant energy out of the field.

For working in meditation, the left side tends to be receptive. If you want to communicate with spirit and receive inspiration, intuition and illumination, put a clear quartz transmitter crystal in your left hand and hold it in-between your heart chakra and your throat chakra, and then send love to it. Placing an opaque, feminine receptive crystal in the right hand will assist in the process. Typically, crystals used like that will amplify the energy about seven times. If you are meditating and you start to feel where your ignorance, avoidance and denial are, it will be seven times more intense if you meditate with a crystal. Feel as you feel without judgment. You can think to yourself, "Ooooh, that feeling is awful" or you can think "Wow, great! Now it will be seven times easier for me to transform that fear into love." It all depends on how you look at it.

You can find more information and you may buy excellent quality crystals already prepared for healing at http://sourcecentre.net.au

Chapter 13
More working with Crystals

~~~

Crystals really enjoy music. Select music to create a subtle, constant fluctuating air pressure to stimulate the piezo electric effect[13], and the crystals will work a lot better. They don't like background noise and chatter.

Have the client lie down preferably on a healing table. Place the female hand crystal in their left hand, point up towards their wrist; and the masculine in their right hand, point down towards their fingers. If the person is not particularly grounded, hold their feet and connect with the planet: feel and know the person to be really grounded. They won't get much out of it if half of them spaces out and floats off. Place your left hand on the soles of their feet, the right hand over the top, and just affirm and feel connection to the planet. It helps to visualise their bodies all centred and connected to the grounding cord. See the top end of the grounding cord going to the centre of all of the bodies.

---

[13] The piezo electric effect is the interaction of mechanical and electrical states within crystalline materials. Essentially, is means that when you apply mechanical stress to a crystal, it generates an electromagnetic field.

Intuitively sense what stones to place on their body. Some stones will almost jump out at you to be used. Using stones from your own continent, or where the person was born, works really well.

Attune to your client and work closely with the crystals. Use your intuition, for each person is unique. Some suggested stones to use for the chakras include:

Chakra level	Colour	Crystal
Base Survival Chakra	Red	Smoky Quartz, Rhodonite, Garnet
Sacral Sexual Chakra	Orange	Carnelian, Citrine, Amber
Solar plexus Personality Chakra	Yellow	Citrine, Topaz, Gold Calcite
Heart Love Chakra	Green	Adventurine, Chrysophrase, Rose Quartz

Throat Communication Chakra	Blue	Celestite, Turquoise, Aquamarine
Brow Knowledge Chakra	Indigo	Lapis Lazuli, Sugilite, Azurite
Crown Spiritual Chakra	Gold and Violet	Clear Quartz, Amethyst

Haematite is excellent to assist both the practitioner and client to be fully present and grounded.

If someone has a migraine, you wouldn't use a masculine crystal for healing because it would probably make their head hurt more. You would use a female crystal to disperse that energy concentration, or to draw the stagnant energy out of their field. As the left side of your body is the receptive side, you would use the female crystal in your left hand for the drawing effect.

Firstly, be very clear with intention to balance and align this person. Attune to the universal energy field and the planet's energy field. Feel into those crystal clusters in the core of the planet. Over time, the intelligence in the crystal you are working with improves at doing its work. It becomes more in its own knowing, and understands how to streamline the healing process.

Place your wand in your right hand and send love to it. Lift it to your chest and feel at your heart and throat the energy coming out of the end of that crystal, to ensure it is transmitting. Then you are ready to start. The left hand crystal is receiving, and the right hand crystal is transmitting.

Working down the front of their body will also extend to and work down the back. Sometimes you will get the message to have the person roll over and do the same process on their back; but most of the time this is unnecessary.

Always start with the crown, a few inches away from the top of the head. You may feel to go out further from the body. Then go in each chakra, and slowly start rotating in a clockwise direction somewhere between where the etheric body starts and the emotional body. You will sense these zones.

In a woman, the energy in the crown (spiritual centre atop the head) generally moves anti-clockwise, and in a man clockwise. It reverses as it moves down each of the chakras (one goes clockwise, the next one anticlockwise and so on). When you start, it is important that you don't go against the flow. It is important to note that in homosexuals the rotation is reversed.

From the feedback you are getting from the left hand, the crystal will direct the right hand. The crystal may want to move, and sometimes it feels like the crystal is running around the rim of a glass. Sometimes it wants to move in strange shapes, in and out. You want the crystal to be happy going around and around in circles. You get to a point where the crystal directs through your nervous system and takes control of your arm. The crystal is an extension of your arm and energy matrix.

With experience, healing becomes intuitive, just like playing a musical instrument. You might feel pressure in your own head, so keep going until that pressure is alleviated. You might feel heat (resistance or blockage); address that area until it feels cool. You might get an intuitive sense for the direction to move in. Some people hear discordant noises in their head until the area is balanced and clear, and then they hear a nice pure tone. There is no right or wrong feedback mechanism. Move with the flow, be connected, holding pure intentions and be open to inspirations.

If there is damage to the etheric body, if the emotional body is really hung up, or if it feels like you are banging against something, or you get stuck like you are in chewing gum… in those situations, keep working in any direction - clockwise or anti-clockwise - until the crystal tells you to move on.

Start on the left and work down each arm. You will find your left hand will look for meridians. When you get to the feet, put your left hand or a female crystal there, and work on both sides of the feet. This is grounding and clearing for the whole system.

Going up and down both sides of the body can take up to 45 minutes, depending on what you find. The crystal may stay in one place, and if you ask the person you may find they had an injury or surgery there. If there has been any major tear or break in the etheric body, it can let in viruses. When you start working on someone that has never had it done before, you will find all sorts of weird and wonderful stuff and it can take an hour.

Watch and see what happens, and you will learn and get a feel for different issues and blockages. You will get a knowing for the best energy for an issue. Observe and be sensitive, rather than read in a book. During a session, make a mental note when something has gone on. After the session, tell 'Upstairs'[14] what occurred; they will be there to share understanding. Over time, you end up with your own unique, seasoned expression, rather than just being cloned as a certain

---

[14] Upstairs is a term for the healing spirits that work with spiritual healers. There are many flavours and grades of these energies and which level works with you depends upon the clarity of your intention and the purity of your motives.

generic type of healer. Wisdom is enhanced from learning from experience. Make your own exploration.

Denied energy gets pushed into the cells. In a healing, it can be pushed back into the chakra system, and up to the heart to be felt and released. To assist this, place a clear Quartz crystal in their left palm chakra, perhaps with a herbal essence or a homeopathic remedy, or anything you feel inspired to.

Place whatever you want to project or transmit in your left hand - for example the sacred quality of courage from blue Tiger Eye - and draw that in through the left side of your body, across your heart, and project it straight into their heart centre through your right hand and crystal. Amethyst resonates at the frequency of the transmuting and transformational violet flame. To assist transformation for the client, direct energy drawn from an Amethyst and project it out through all of their chakras. This also tends to release energy in their etheric or physical body that has been denied. Gently wash this transformational energy through their whole field and then, as much as they may want to, that energy cannot be denied. To help the person ground and connect, take the Haematite and draw that energy in, and project it through the lower chakras.

Run your hands fairly close to the client's body and feel if it is an even temperature, or warm or cool. If you feel a major area of temperature change, then there is more work to be done. The person may be in denial of something and they will tuck it somewhere, and then move it around their body to try to hide it from you. Feel into your own body, and if it doesn't feel quite right, you might do more.

When you are finished, seal their aura by using your right hand to trace an infinity symbol over their field, a number of times, centring on the navel area. Finish by just holding their feet and loving and accepting them.

Crystal healing is an amazing therapy with profound effects, particularly when used in combination with fresh herbs, homeopathic remedies, herbal essences and COSMOSIS® elixirs directed into the client's chakras. The healing effect lasts until the next full moon. As soon as the moon starts to wane, the healing effect dissipates. Hopefully, the client will maintain the healing and make changes in their behaviour to hold these new levels of wholeness. A healer can facilitate certain healing effects, but it is the choice and responsibility of the client to move into a new style of functioning. We do not *heal* anyone, we are simply part of the mechanism of healing.

At the Cosmosis® Mentoring Centre we offer courses in Seership and Crystal healing.

More information at http://mysteryschool.org.au

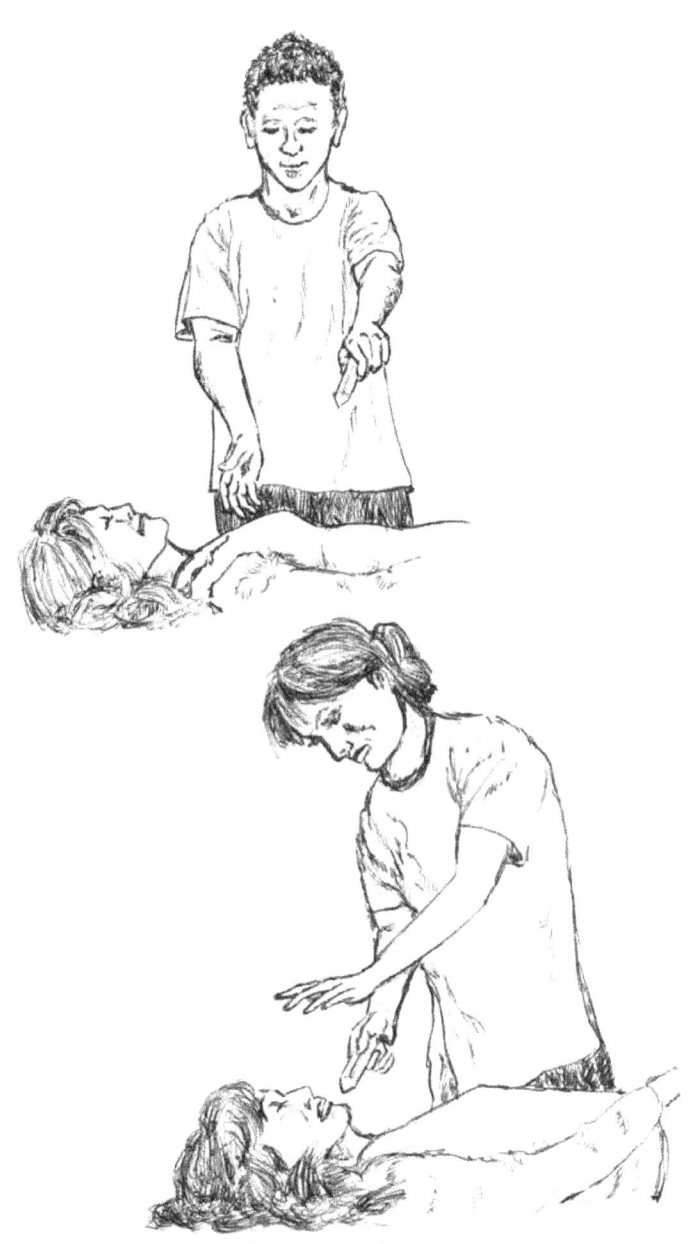

Crystal healing

Chapter 14
Planetary Healing and Rituals

~~~

This alchemical healing ritual attunes you to the universal energies, which are being directed towards the Earth to heal and restore harmony to our beloved sphere. As we serve as the channel for these healing energies, so do we also over time, transform ourselves into beings of love, enlightenment and wisdom. It works with the spiritual energies which condition and guide the evolution of consciousness upon this planet during the coming age. It is also beneficial for clearing and healing the chakras and associated endocrine glands.

Start by sitting upright or laying down in a comfortable position, in a relaxed bodily state. You may wish to play some quiet music to assist you to create a feeling of peace. If you have a clear Quartz crystal, place it in your left hand and hold it in the region of your higher heart/throat chakras. The crystal will serve to amplify and intensify the healing effect of this meditation.

N.B. Remember to cleanse your crystals at least weekly, as they tend to accumulate disharmonious energies over time.

Close your eyes and visualise yourself way out in space, orbiting the planet, looking down upon the Earth spinning upon its axis. Open your heart and visualise a beam of pure white spiritual light emanating from the centre of your brow, and shining down upon the Earth. Combine and merge this light with a feeling and stream of rose-pink unconditional love welling up from your heart centre, totally encapsulating the planet. See any darkened areas upon the planet beginning to light up as you feel the Earth being freed from fear.

Focus this light, charged with unconditional love, healing and nurturing all of the kingdoms upon the planet one by one: the mineral kingdom, the devic kingdom, the plant kingdom, the animal kingdom, the kingdom of humanity and the kingdom of souls. Relate now in loving enlightenment with all of the kingdoms, each with its own equally important and necessary role within the scheme of All That Is, All that will be and has been upon the planet.

Say to yourself, MAY LOVE RESTORE THE BALANCE

Focus that love and light on anyone you know who is in need of healing, or on any situation, circumstance, or fellow being with whom there is ill feeling. This reduces, and ultimately eliminates, any negative energy flowing towards you, and frees you from the chains of the past. Will yourself to send this love unconditionally, without expectation of return or agenda. All of this energy ultimately returns to you as healing energy and enlightenment. As it balances the conflict within you that is reflected upon the planet, so will it return to you as nurturing, supportive energies for your own growth.

Say to yourself, MAY LOVE RESTORE THE BALANCE

Repeat the affirmation:

I call upon the spirits of love and light to stand guard at the doorway to my soul. Protect me from the forces of darkness and deception, and guide me upon the pathway of love, light and truth.

I now commit myself to the light.

Source is within all that is, Source is within me, Source within grow strong.

Now you become aware that you are entirely surrounded by a vibrant living flame of Violet light. This is the transformational energy of nature which allows metamorphosis. Its purifying, refining action cleanses you of that which prevents you from freely expressing your true essence. As you look down, the Violet Flame also surrounds and pervades the entire planet, and all of its being-ness. Hold this awareness of the planet and all it contains bathing, purifying, refining and cleansing. After several minutes of holding this image and feeling, consciously direct the flame to any trouble spots on the planet surface, such as sites of military conflict and environmental catastrophe. See and *feel* this conflict resolving into *harmony*. The Violet Flame energy cleanses, aligns and purifies the conflict upon the planet, so we may enter into an age of enlightenment, free from the intense competitive struggle for existence. See and feel this transformation.

Say to yourself, MAY LOVE RESTORE THE BALANCE

From out in space, concentrate the flame and send it down to yourself on the planet surface. Draw the flame down into each chakra in turn.

Draw the flame in through the crown chakra (spiritual centre) - high atop the head - and flowing into the head area, activating, cleansing and harmonising where there is conflict within you. Direct the Violet Flame especially into the pineal gland, which is the physical externalisation of the crown chakra.

Say to yourself, MAY LOVE RESTORE THE BALANCE.

Draw it in through the brow chakra (knowledge centre) – in the centre of the brow - flooding the head and neck areas, aligning the brow with the crown chakra, so that these two centres may work in loving unison to ground and express illumination, inspiration and an intuitive knowing. Draw it particularly into the pituitary and hypothalamus glands, the externalisations of the brow chakra.

Say to yourself, MAY LOVE RESTORE THE BALANCE

Draw the Violet Flame in through the throat chakra (communication centre), at the base of the throat. This is the seat of our communication ability, and our ability to express love and higher creative energy in all its forms. Draw the energy into the thyroid gland in the neck. Relate with that creativity as the Violet Flame flows through this centre, and feel your entire body being inspired to lead a life of love and wisdom.

Say to yourself, MAY LOVE RESTORE THE BALANCE.

Now draw the Violet Flame in through the heart chakra (love centre) in the middle of the chest, and feel the heart centre expand and awaken to the feeling of unconditional love. Direct the violet flame into the thymus gland in the chest. Now cycle the Violet Flame up to the (brow chakra) hypothalamus and pituitary glands through the (throat chakra) thyroid gland. Feel the Violet Flame linking these centres and aligning the soul with its physical representative. Feel your heart being cleansed of suffering and the pain you have accumulated on your journey through eternity. Surrender to the love you feel and release any judgment that arises.

Say to yourself, IN OF AND FOR LOVE, MAY THE LOVING VIOLET FLAME RESTORE THE BALANCE

Draw that Violet Flame now in through the solar plexus chakra and into the pancreas, this is the seat of the lower will, the personality. It is the focus for the tension between the soul and its personality. The will expressed through this centre is the collective desire nature and intent of the mental processes of the lower mind; it is not a spiritual reality. This is a reflection of how you choose to focus your energy with your thoughts, deeds and emotions. Cleanse this centre now, and open it up to the unconditional love of the playful, serene, spiritual being which you are in essence.

Say to yourself, MAY LOVE RESTORE THE BALANCE

Draw that Violet Flame in now through the sacral chakra (sexual centre), in the region of the navel. This is the seat of the desire nature, of ambition, of 'I want' regardless of the consequences or harm caused. To live a truly spiritual life of love, the soul must direct the flow of creativity from this centre up through the heart centre and into the throat chakra. The sacral energies must become subordinate to the loving expression of the creative spiritual Will of your eternal being. Feel the Violet Flame cleanse the gonads which are linked to this centre.

Say to yourself, MAY LOVE RESTORE THE BALANCE

Draw that Violet Flame now up through the base chakra (survival centre), and cleanse all insecurities you may feel arise. Feel the Violet Flame flood through the adrenal glands which are the physical expression of the base chakra. Feel the flame flood now out into the entire bloodstream, and cleanse the physical body of judgment and disharmonies. The base chakra is our link to Earth: become one with the essence of the planet. Feel that Violet Flame now flowing up into you from within the very heart of the planet.

Say to yourself MAY LOVE RESTORE THE BALANCE

Feel now the flame moving up and out into the subtle bodies of the auric field. Feel the flame flooding into and cleansing the physical-etheric, emotional, mental and soul bodies.

Direct the Violet Flame to any point of disharmony within your physical body. The love of the planet flows through you. The love of the cosmos, to whatever measure you allow, now flows through you.

As you stand poised on that middle-point between Heaven and Earth, so are you content to discover, create and love your destiny. Yet you may still aspire and dream, dreams woven into a tapestry of love, and that LOVE NOW RESTORES THE BALANCE.

Let us now affirm to the universe that which we are in essence. Let us invoke the help and support of those higher beings motivated by love, guided by enlightenment, those who seek to inspire and activate a fully realised understanding of that which we are, and our path within the plan of Creation.

Seek now to relate with a subtle reality beyond the physical form. Seek to still the mind, and enter into a loving, nurturing communion with the energies, and the understanding which may flow through you and guide your every action and your very understanding, in of and for Love.

Become that Love. Be aware of what you feel within your body. Choose joy and bliss as a state of being. Choose to surrender the vain illusionary desires of the three-fold personality, and embrace your spiritual reality free from the distortions associated with the temporal forms of sensibility of time and space.

Choose to simply now BE.

Repeat this affirmation:

I AM,

I AM All That I AM,

One with the universal mind,

One with the Source of all life,

I AM one with all life forms and they are one with me.

I AM love, I AM light, I AM truth, I AM peace.   *I AM*

In that which I AM, I call for the protection and guidance of the spirits of love, light and truth, from the higher mental plane and beyond, and I refuse all communications which originate upon the astral (emotional) plane.

I AM.

Within the body, feel lighter and encapsulated in Love.

Say to yourself MAY LOVE RESTORE THE BALANCE.

Now see yourself surrounded by a protective nurturing sheath like a cloak, tinged with deep royal blue. All of your energy centres are functioning harmoniously. Feeling more stable now, return to normal consciousness, enhanced by light, love and peace.

About *RITUALS*

What is truly good ritual work? It is when people have spiritualised their egos to such a degree that they surrender in, of and for love to greater forces at work, and they come out transformed in various degrees as a result. But the beauty is that, in and during the process, they have something uniquely valuable to offer from their hearts.

I have mixed feelings about what have traditionally been known as rituals. The problem with rituals is that they spin out energy from your *personal* centre; so if your own life is not together, then all you spin out into the world is the magnified disharmony of your own life.

The most valuable aspect of your work for the planet and beyond is the love that you have to offer to people, and your energy while you are in such a loving state. It is all about harmony in your personal sphere.

Although I continue to work on my own issues, I have been able to accomplish a lot. This is because there has been relative harmony on the levels I was working on, as well as a shared commitment and vision within my inner and outer relationships.

There are issues, and there are ISSUES. If people do not get their foundation sorted out - like clearing the fear in their egos and psyches to a certain degree, and not being run by their lower animals nature - then all they can imprint into the world through rituals are more distortions and fear based contaminations.

Many people tell me that a minimum standard of clarity and purity is not required to do spiritual work, but certainly the evidence is to the contrary. Over and over, I have seen skilled, grounded spiritual leaders who are able to hold their own energies in clarity and purity have their spiritual work fall apart, because the people associated with them do not get their foundational work in order. If people get in touch with their inner creativity but then operate through the un-clarity and fear in their psyche, then all they may create is more un-clarity and fear.

It does not matter how pure a mountain spring is at its source….. if the channel you use to pipe that water to its destination is contaminated so then will the water arrive at its destination contaminated. It is the same with spiritual work. It matters not whether you are doing healing, teaching, psychic reading or whatever, if you as the channel have not cleared out your own fear and judgment so then will all of your spiritual work arrive at its destination contaminated and corrupt.

Not one group, as yet, has successfully anchored and actualised the new paradigm ideals for this new age. This is not to say that there is not good work being done, of course there is. But unless a minimum standard of clarity and purity is adhered to, then the long-term effects on the collective consciousness are just more distortions being added, which will need to be cleaned up in future moments. Without an ongoing serious daily commitment to psychological clearing practices, this will not change.

I have often seen and heard of so-called 'powerful transformations' in groups. Everyone present has a huge realisation in the moment, but the actual change in their behaviour, thought-patterns and the releasing of judgments that follows is invariably near to zero. So, how can anyone say there has been a powerful transformation in a group when there is no fundamental change in behaviour produced as a result?

My biggest concern, on a global scale, is the commonly held idea that you can realise God (Source) without any fundamental change in behaviour. You only transform the world by fundamentally living the ideal in your own life, to the best of your ability. All over the world there are spiritual groups leading self indulgent hedonistic lifestyles believing themselves to be somehow better than everyone else….. with their own little monopoly on truth and the only guru that is the true this or that. It would be laughable if it were not such a sad phenomenon.

I have never witnessed a ritual that propelled anyone into major realignment of their personality life with the inner truth of the human spirit; not unless there was an ongoing prior commitment to the practice of egoless-ness – real, demonstrated and expressed in the day-to-day livings.

People sit around in groups doing all kinds of rituals with no real understanding of what they are doing, creating the most hideous forms in the ethers, and driving all the nature spirits away. They go away feeling great, and fluff themselves up about what great work they are doing.

I could assemble the best heavy metal musicians to play a Baroque opera led by the best conductor in the world, and it would still be horrible because the 'ritual' would not have been performed correctly. It would not have been performed with the correct understanding, discipline nor insight. So how are other rituals any different?

Great rituals not only need a great leader. All the participants also need to be clear in their intent, and have a certain degree of purity of heart for the evoked effect to be positive, constructive and lasting. Anything that works through them is affected by the clarity of their own channels; without clarity the ritual is prone to do more harm than good.

In ancient times, people completed twenty one years of training before they could perform rituals on behalf of the populace. If you open to spirit prematurely - *as often happens with drug use or rituals* - then the spiritual currents become subverted to the lower desire nature, and all this does is energise the ego. That is the danger of ritual.

Aquarius, the coming age is an age of insight. Rituals seldom produce genuine insight, and therefore seldom assist enlightenment. Rituals, as they are being performed by and large, are 'old age'. To be harnessed effectively, the whole ritual movement must be brought into line with the science of invocative decree[15]. With a few small modifications to their procedure, most spells or rituals could be increased in efficiency a thousandfold. I love being a student and gaining greater insight. When I meet someone who is a master of something, I gratefully take instruction. This quality seems to be lost in the many these days.

You know, if the planet was miraculously healed tomorrow, it would be a galactic disaster because of the symbiotic nature of things. Nothing is in isolation. The whole system must be healed in stages and in a specific order, otherwise lots of things are thrown out of balance in a chain reaction of homeostatic chaos.

You wouldn't take a starving refugee to MacDonald's and stuff them full of hamburgers. Rather, you'd wean them back onto food over a period of time to allow their digestive

---

[15] The science of invocative decree is an alchemical understanding which attunes ones intention, motivation and actions to the agreed goals and levels of the Earth within the creative plan

enzymes to reform, and for the whole system to heal and adapt to the increased energy.

What I see are many well-intentioned sincere people, with little understanding of how the cosmos works, madly creating more imbalances out of a misguided sense of urgency. There is no urgency; there is simply a need for harmony, and only harmony leads to more harmony.

There is nothing wrong with anything, there is just disharmony. Create harmony, and then allow that to ripple out into the universe: *this is the only wise use of ritual.*

Using ritual to work our little wills, and heal specific things that we judge to be wrong or broken, is the height of folly.

Rituals can only help if the foundational practices are in place. To spearhead global change, we require clarity. It assists not at all to come from a sense of urgency, or in other words fear.

There are many people whose specific mission it is to raise awareness about global new paradigm issues however almost all of these are still trying to skip steps in their own actualisation processes.

For many of you, your personal lives are still a bit messy (I am being kind). You need to free yourselves from the fear based patterning and programming in your ego and psyche. You need to manifest harmony in your personal sphere, and to lose all victim consciousness. Only then can you start looking at being a major influence for good in the world.

Harmony and enlightenment are first generated at home. All any of us can produce in the world is what we have at home. Unless your private life is reflecting the order and harmony we seek in the world at large, all you can do on a grander level is produce more of what you have at home. So let's concentrate on first cleaning up our own backyards before we embark on any crusades.

If there is one thing I fully understand, it is that there is nothing wrong with anything. Most people feel very uncomfortable in disharmony and so want harmony - and this is where we focus. I don't want to arrogantly heal the Earth now at all costs. I want to listen to her, resonate with her great guiding spirit, and act from that space because she knows what she needs.

Similarly, I don't want anyone telling me what I need, and what to do about what I need. I don't want ready-made answers on how things are, and I don't want ancient maps of initiation or an imposed futuristic vision. However, such is probably the present service profile of many of people who are out there working as spiritual teachers.

I myself have had the good fortune to participate in many collective rituals over many lifetimes with truly excellent leaders, who knew how to guide people into spirit communion. The results were always pure magic and deeply transformational work. All of us really connected from the heart; that's what sacred space is. Our rituals were very subtle, and within them we were guided to design our own preferred ways of journeying with spirit.

After participating in these rituals, I came to face and harmonise masses of issues in my own backyard, but it was the best thing that could have ever happened to me. It doesn't mean that before this clearing I was not able to contribute some light to the planet however they massively increased the efficacy of everything I be and do. Those rituals worked for me in those moments because of the clarity and purity of the leader, the absence of any agenda about attempting to force healing upon something outside of ourselves judged to be 'broken', and because all the participants were adequately prepared by clearing their fears.

I strongly feel that the face of teaching and learning is transforming. In future moments there will be no 'need' and there will be nothing to teach in the way it is now understood. There will only be a dance between communion and communication, between all of us and the planet. Some of us are afraid to dance, jumping on one leg only. We are all a little lame, battered, hurt, wounded and imperfect. But Love does not require a perfect form nor a perfect psyche; it simply needs to flow and be allowed to express itself as love. The trick is to learn how to get out of your own way so that whatever wounded-ness you carry does not distort the expression of that love in any way. Acceptance, allowance, tolerance and humility are the key elements involved.

Ponder upon this understanding for it contains the keys to the new knowings which shall lead you into the portal of alchemical transformation.

Chapter 15

The COSMOSIS® Process for Transformational Healing

What is Cosmosis®?

Cosmosis® is an internal process for personal growth that enables you to change how you respond to the world. This personal growth process changes your personal reactions and feelings about the people and situations in your life, and, instead of simply reacting to life, empowers you to consciously choose how you respond. It transforms your old programming and fear-based belief systems. The process has nothing to do with anyone or anything else, it's just self meeting self, time and time again until you get the message that everything in your environment is a reflection of you, and that your life is your creation.

As you change your personal response to the people and situations you have attracted to yourself, your journey through life improves. It is very easy to measure your change because the people and situations pressing your buttons will suddenly appear to be acting differently, and your buttons won't get pressed in the same way anymore. This is because the relationship dynamics in your life have been transformed.

As you use the process more, you will become more aware of your feelings and they will become increasingly heightened. This is progress, it is a sign that you are ready to transmute all feelings – both painful and enjoyable - that you have been avoiding and denying.

Feelings are your soul's experience of the totality of your existence as a human being; it is the soul that feels. Everything you perceive - all of your sensations (physical/etheric and spiritual bodies), emotions and thoughts enable your soul to feel.

It is important to let go of anticipated outcomes in any transformational process. Your infinite healing intelligence decides what shifts first. Change doesn't always happen in the order or the way your mind wants it to occur. However, you will be delighted with the speed of your accelerated growth.

In the beginning, you might only release one layer at a time around a particular issue. Very quickly, you will gain the competence to release multiple layers at once and work at deeper levels.

Each person's experience of the Cosmosis® process will be personal and individual. You may feel anything from hot to cold, lightness, relaxation, relief, heightened awareness, aliveness, and much more, as the energy moves through your energy matrix. Shifts will become more pronounced as you progress.

Alchemy is a process of transmutation. Transmutation is about transforming a substance/energy into a higher, purer and finer vibration. For instance: lead into gold, fear into love.

Love and Fear are not opposites; they are the same energy vibrating at different frequencies. Just like hot and cold on the thermometer are not really opposites, they are simply the same energy vibrating at different levels. Fear is not energised from Source or spirit; we keep it energised through our habits and choices.

The Cosmosis® process assists you to transmute any low vibration energy into higher vibration energy. Transmutation creates genetic changes at cellular level. This alchemical process is the central tenet of Cosmosis®.

Any issue you encounter is there because you have a judgment. The steps are about aligning your bodies so that the energy trapped by that judgment may be released back to the correct place in the space/time continuum - which is at the precise moment the judgment first occurred.

When you judge something, you attach yourself to it and start dragging it along with you from one moment to another. This is why you feel out of place and things don't feel right: because you are dragging misplaced energy along with you. You restore harmony by allowing the misplaced energy to return to its correct place in space and time.

This process is a conscious choice, and it is in your power to choose how your various bodies - tangible and subtle - resonate in all moments.

Cosmosis® is easy to use and does not require any bodily movements, tools or other props. All you need is yourself, the will to move beyond your present conditioned limits, and the desire to embrace more love. The Cosmosis® process has been thoroughly designed and developed to ensure that anyone willing to let go of old baggage, and applying the steps correctly, is able to expand into more of their true potential.

A major focus of our training is gaining psychological clarity. What does that mean? It means clearing out all old fear-based patterning and programming from our psyches. This is all the things we have taken on board, which have limited us in some way, and has kept us from seeing the Truth and the Knowing of our own hearts. In working on gaining psychological clarity, we regain our individual sovereignty: we are not controlled by anyone or anything external to ourselves. We are then free to hear the voice of our own heart, to hear our own Truth within, to hear the voice of spirit and connect with Source ourselves.

Many people settle for mediocrity in life. This path is not for those people. This path is for those of you who wish to be truly outstanding individuals in a sea of mediocrity, to seize the day and actualise the greatness that you inherently hold within, as a human spirit.

As you work through the processes and lessons of this path, you will be uncovering the true You - your authentic self. This is the gift that you are then able to take out into the world and share with others. It is envisaged that you will be able to teach others psychological clarity, sharing the gifts and creating a world of unity, harmony and unconditional love.

Imagine a world where all people live in harmony, everyone on a voyage of self discovery – each supporting the other, lovingly. The Truth is prized and 'success' has a new meaning. Imagine a world in which the predominant thinking is in the spirit of "Let us co-create..." instead of "I want..." Imagine being inspired and inspiring. Through our training programs, let us co-create this new world of equality, unity and harmony, with courage and joy.

We understand it can be challenging to discern the truth from illusion and to make the leap from the familiar to the unknown... To trust we are safe to explore new ways, to expand our focus and awareness, to see the world and all her colours with fresh eyes, and truly be a part of the transformation that is occurring right here, right now. You do have the courage within you to make this change.

Are you ready?

The time of Transformation is here now if you but choose!

The Cosmosis® Steps

There are 10 steps in the process. Please appreciate that this is a very basic introduction to this process. If you want to apply it seriously, then the purpose is to get to experience, understand and embody each step as a process in itself on all levels of your being. It is not something that you head trip or just feel in your heart. Rather, it must be a holistic experience - a way of being and living - which includes a fundamental choice and reorientation to engage in the culture of love in your life, on all levels.

The 10 steps

1. Align
2. Centre
3. Allow
4. Feel
5. Acknowledge
6. Gratitude
7. Release Judgment
8. Re-choose

9. Release

10. Harmonise

What is Energy healing?

Energy healing usually involves some conscious use of knowledge of the human energy field, as well as specific techniques to address disturbances. Programs which are based on the medical model will have an assessment of the energy field, and techniques will be chosen that address the disturbances found. After the energy healing is done, the healer would re-assess the field to discover the outcome of the treatment.

What is Spiritual Healing?

Traditionally, spiritual healing is healing in which the healer is felt to be an instrument of the divine, allowing the power of the divine to heal through him or her. The healer acknowledges that he or she does not do the healing. In a sense, the healer is only the instrument through which the person seeking healing surrenders to the divine.

COSMOSIS® Transformational Healing has aspects of both energy and spiritual healing, as well as involving training, mentoring, coaching, counselling, introspection and self awareness techniques. The fundamental basis for Cosmosis® transformational healing is to embrace a working hypothesis, which states that we are all from the same Source, and so fundamentally are all aspects of that one Source. Our understanding holds that it is self-evident that the body, mind and spirit are interconnected and inseparable. And since our aura (the human energy field) interacts with others, as well as with this spiritual whole, so all of our actions, beliefs and thoughts do affect that whole.

From this understanding, we choose to accept that we are all part of a greater interconnected benevolent being-ness, and learn to exercise healthy boundaries based upon a personal preference for ever greater love, wisdom, tolerance and contentment, through service to that spiritual whole.

The resulting belief structure becomes the lens through which healing and enlightenment occurs. Within this process, there is an absence of the rather ugly dogmatic bias which characterises some other schools of philosophy and religiosity. The Cosmosis® personal development /enlightenment process is a systematic identification with this greater being-ness, which translates to greater understanding, wisdom and love. This then flows on into behaviour change, as we learn together to engage in a true culture of love, tolerance and wisdom. The more we act out of this understanding, the more we are freed from the 'Thou Shalts' we have been carrying around with us. Ultimately, through dedication and hard work with this process of self-awareness and expansion of consciousness, we personally effect our own investigation of the 'truth'. We learn to become expressions of our own Source on the planet, and to the planet.

The major potential pitfall in this process (or any spiritual process for that matter) is what I term the 'more spiritual than thou syndrome'. Spiritual pride - feeling you are 'better than' or more 'entitled to' because you are on the spiritual path - only serves to limit you to being so much less than your potential.

We by no means testify that this is the only way to enlightenment. It is but one way, which you may choose if it resonates as relevant for you. It does give consistent and duplicatable results, and we have a Medical Doctor, Psychologist, Naturopath and Holistic Counsellors on staff overseeing our training. All of our mentors and coaches have fully government-accredited qualifications and most are multi-modality healing practitioners in their own rights.

How to transform fear into unconditional love, joy, lightness and limitlessness -- allowing your heart to sing with Cosmosis®...

Ten Simple Steps

THE ALCHEMICAL KEYS TO SELF-TRANSCENDENCE, INTEGRATED ASCENSION AND SELF-MASTERY.

There is no such thing as good or bad energy. When, however, energy is displaced from its original place within the space-time continuum, and has none of its natural counter-balances from that home moment, things start to go awry.

The plan for this planet is to create equality, where men and women of different races and religions walk hand in hand, honouring differences within sameness. The Earth has learned from the fear that has existed here for a long time. She is over it and would like to experience something else.

Karma is the balance between love and fear. Everything that we do, think, and feel adds to the total amount of fear or love on this planet. Persistent indulging in fear and victimhood keeps us stuck. The degree of resistance we have to embracing, embodying and being the truth is the degree to which we are attached to maintaining our condition, limit and fear.

The simple secret of Cosmosis® is: to transmute something we just raise its vibration. This process is a conscious choice. When fear is loved hard, it melts. Fear is just frozen love, a lower vibrational state of love. Cosmosis® raises fear through the conditional states of love, into unconditional love and beyond. Most ones on the spiritual path are apologetic about their light, fearing the possible consequences of fully being the light and sharing their love. We have been conditioned from childhood to believe that to love ourselves is bad. There is no good or bad energy; there are simply choices and consequences.

We can simply choose how our bodies resonate in all moments. We have the ability to be in control of our entire energy matrix in all moments, in of and for love, in service to All That Is. We can get rid of the voices in our head, unconscious and subconscious fears, and inner critic. Fear is not energised from Source or spirit. We keep it energised through our habits and choices.

When the energy of joy is lowered in frequency, we become less giving, more paranoid, more introspective and even depressed. We can experience hopelessness, separateness and victim consciousness. If the energy plummets deep enough, we can experience despair.

We use an enormous amount of our energy to self-contract, self-limit and self-condition with our attachments, avoidance and denial. When we stop doing that, we free up energy so we can really make a difference and move mountains!

We can choose to resonate at higher frequencies where there is the quality of openness, a feeling of empowerment, connectedness, allowing-ness and an absence of fear.

"I choose to be liberated in unconditional love and non-attachment, so I may anchor and bring the highest and most radiant light into this realm. I now choose and will towards walking the talk as a human being, and being clear and bright in all moments."

Step 1. Align

A lot of times, we desire to know the truth provided the truth is "this" or "that". This is different to just wanting to accept the truth unconditionally, without wanting to colour or change it. It is one thing to want to accept the truth as an intellectual necessity; it is another to really desire to *know* the truth.

When we emanate from Source and step down and out into form, we maintain a connection to Source. Our journey of return, and the ascension process, is geared around building an inter-dimensional bridge of awareness back to Source. We build this through intention, and by embodying Source purity. This allows the ascension column to manifest, and from it we can feed the three-fold flame of love, wisdom and power within our heart centre.

Visualise and feel this ascension column between your heart and Source, through all the levels of self and spirit, connecting you into the highest, clearest, most loving light. Allow this column to ground through you into the core of the Earth, grounding your connection to Source and spirit presence here and now on the planet, fully present.

Call forth a personal, planetary and universal axiatonal alignment. Consciously seek that re-connection with Source, anchored in the heart. Choose to act as a free creative agent, grounding and expressing love energy from Source to spiritualise matter. Affirm and choose to remember that this is what you are about. Align with planetary plan and purpose, and your incarnational blueprint[16], and ask for the Circle of Sirius to support you in your journey.

---

[16] This is predetermined by the choices previously made in conjunction with the direction the soul is heading (destiny). To some degree it sets the scope of the incarnation, contains karmic limitations and also sets up the magnetic attractions and repulsions which predispose the soul to react to certain stimuli in certain ways to evolve towards its destiny.

I am Affirmation

I AM, I Am All That I AM

One with the universal mind, One with the Source of all life. I AM One with all life forms and they are one with me. I AM Love, I AM light, I AM truth, I AM peace.

I AM

I AM a conscious, concentrated point of living light within the macrocosm, through which energy is focused; and in, of and for love, I choose to love and love I will.

I AM.

In that which I AM, I now call forth the protection and guidance of the spirits of love, light and truth from the higher mental planes and beyond; and I refuse all communications which originate upon the emotional plane.

I AM.

In that which I AM, I now call forth and accept a deep penetration of the light of All That Is, thereby allowing a full and open radiation of my entire energy matrix, in service to All That Is.

I AM

Step 2. Centre

Feel and know yourself as a spot within the macrocosm through which energy is focused, a conscious conductor of living energy. Feel your grounding cord between your heart and the Earth's heart centre, and keep your connection to the planet through your feet open, to maintain your connection with the Earth. Be in your body. Feel the flesh, bones, organs and circulatory system with blood coursing through it. Feel into the heart and lungs area. As you breathe, feel the air going into the lungs, transferring life into your blood stream, bringing nutrients and sustenance to the cells.

Feel and put awareness into your heart centre to balance your expression of love, wisdom and power. See the pillar or column of light/love that extends way up through your head, crown and soul star (a centre of energy above the head), and reaches down through your Earth star (the energy centre under your feet), anchoring into the heart of Mother Earth. See all your bodies centred over your heart, and regularly flood them with violet transforming light - the Violet Flame. Call forth gold and platinum nets to move through your energy system, clearing all imbalanced energies. See a rainbow of spiralling energy sweep through the physical, emotional, mental and lower spiritual bodies.

When we align, centre and clear the four lower bodies of our energy field (physical, emotional, mental and soul bodies), we begin to feel a sense of calm assurance. We create a smoothness and equalisation of vibration/frequency throughout these bodies. When we are centred and aligned, regardless of what's going on in our environment, we don't resonate in sympathy with any fear. We remain in the 'eye of the storm'.

Aligning and centring enables our bodies and energy channels on all levels to 'click' back into place and be connected, allowing energy to flow freely again. We have to be aligned and centred, because misplaced energy might be in the mental body when it is meant to be in the emotional body. If the bodies are not all aligned - and the dimensional states of each of the various bodies vibrating in harmony - we can intend to release misplaced energy and for that energy to go back to where it is supposed to be in space-time, but it cannot. This is because the connections are not all lined up. Our intention drives the energy, but if it reaches a block, it will end up stuck somewhere in the physical body. If we do that, a lot of organs will eventually break down.

Set an intention to be aware, and remember that all our energy has an effect, and we are responsible for that effect.

Once we are aligned, and then release any judgment, energy will move back to where it belongs. If we hang on to the past, we will drag it along with us and it will slow us down. If we stop hanging on with our judgment and attachment, the past returns to the past and we are free to move forward. Healing occurs simply when displaced energy within the space-time continuum returns to where it belongs. When we align the bodies and open the channels, energy knows where it is meant to be, and it will move there naturally. If we stop hanging onto the energy - which judgment does - and let it go, it will just go home. Over time this process of healing removes faulty belief systems from the mental body, and disharmony in the physical body.

"I am aligned, centred, balanced, powerful and loving in each and every moment"

Step 3. Allow

Simply be. To allow is not thinking about being, or thinking about being a being. Allowance is an absence of attachment, striving and urgency. It is allowing the Spiritual Source within you to shine. In order to allow, we must be free from the desire of approval from others. If we desire the approval of egos, we will not allow truth and love to radiate from within to without. Our primary concern will be about the recognition and approval from egos around us, which has nothing to do with love.

Draw courage, and allow the love from within the heart centre to radiate throughout the four-body system. Surrender to the heart any behaviour that does not express who we truly are. Surrender thoughts of limitation or separation, any resistance, judgment and fear, and allow the warmth of the heart to transform this energy. Rather than looking outside for approval or validation, surrender to the vast potential of heart knowing. Be open and love the truth. Be open to being a vessel for life, love and healing. Be the spot within the macrocosm through which energy is focused, and be conscious and aware of that energy. Simply allow yourself to be as you truly are, here and now, warts and all. Be open to failings and strengths.

The truth simply is and exists whether we want to acknowledge it or not. The Source within only resonates with truth, and is simply covered up with layers of untruth. This recognition sets us free from condition and limit.

"I allow myself to simply be as I truly am, right here, right now. I surrender to grounding love in each and every moment."

Step 4. Feel

Feelings are the truth. By choosing to acknowledge and integrate feelings, we have the truth. If we do not acknowledge the truth, we are left with only lies.

When any manifestation of fear comes up, we choose to know we don't need it any more; it no longer serves us. We feel and love it, but don't judge it or wallow in it. We accept that it is something we created, and now we choose something different. As soon as we stop judging it, no matter how intense, its stored energy will be depleted.

Feel into any fear within the soft tissues of your cellular structure, and the most intense long-term ancestral programming within the skeleton. Feel into any incident when you really admired someone, wanted to be like them, emulated them, and later you realised they had a dark side. Get in touch with and feel all that. It could be a step-parent you have had, a teacher... anyone. We all made choices to survive in a world of egos and have copied patterns from others. Give permission for anything that you have absorbed through giving your power away to others, to be felt and experienced. You may experience elation, relief, joy, lightness, letting go or a release from allowing this feeling. Yet it is not about the phenomena or drama of feeling. It is about allowing yourself to honestly and genuinely experience it all, as it truly feels, without expectations of how that should be. Embrace the whole feeling. Feel as you feel without judgment, and realise you are ready to choose something different.

"I feel as I feel without judgment" "I am the master of my programming and patterning"

Step 5. Acknowledge

Acknowledgment allows us to perceive our feelings and issues for what they really are, as well as see their effect on us and in our life.

Once we truly acknowledge our subconscious and unconscious fear-based patterns and programming, and how that personifies and projects into our life, then we can disempower them. Our fear-based patterns and programs are not who we truly are; they are something we created. Once acknowledged, they no longer control us. This allows us to take responsibility for our part in creating these issues through our judgment. When we take responsibility, we empower ourselves. If we created the issues, we can un-create them. Acknowledgment allows us to transform fear energy into love.

"I have a mind, yet I am not my mind!"

"I have emotions, yet I am not my emotions!"

"I acknowledge how I feel and am. I choose to be the truth"

"I, the creator of this dysfunction, am able to un-create it"

Step 6. Gratitude

Be grateful for the lessons we learn, and for the being we are and will be. It is important to release any judgment associated with people from whom we have copied patterns, or who we perceive as having 'wronged' us. They were and are in their own stage of growth, and carry their own set of issues. Forgive yourself for wanting to emulate anyone who was not worthy of emulation. There is a huge gift in having the choice of how much condition and limit you experience. Be grateful for any realisation of weakness, in order to clear and transform them into strengths. Be grateful for opportunities to see the truth. Any realisation of an issue is an opportunity to heal and let go. Be thankful for the learning and opportunity to express mastery and to grow. Life challenges are the mechanism through which we are stretched and grow, in order to actualise more of our true potential. People, circumstances, places, events that we could choose to judge are our master-teachers. Be really grateful to them for the teaching and opportunity to learn. Gratitude manifests abundance. Any blessing can become a disaster, and any disaster can be turned into a blessing.

"I am grateful for the experience of life itself"

"Source is within All That IS, Source is within me, Source within grow strong"

7. Release judgment

Any memories of actions - past, present or future - which we judged as wrong or inappropriate must be released. We live in an age where judgment and criticism are taught and prized. Receptivity and qualities that nurture are not highly regarded.

It is important that we move beyond judgment. If we judge anything, we choose to not understand or have insight into it. But, for most of us, our favourite pastime is judging things: 'this is right' 'this is wrong'. Most people think that when they stop deciding that everything is evil, wrong or bad, they have moved beyond judgment. All they have really done is shift focus and decided things are good. Through inference, they are still judging things to be bad. Good can only exist in relation to bad, and vice-versa.

In judging the conflict that currently exists between certain ethnic groups, races, religious orientations and ideologies, we create more conflict. You cannot win a war on terror with bombs and guns. You win a war on terror by winning the minds and the hearts of the enemy, and so making them your friends. Judgment gives energy to that which it judges. What we judge, we create and become. However, if we feel and empathise with those groups on a planetary level and feel - in our heart - ways that those currently conflicted energies could harmonise, we will then create more harmony.

The action of judgment is not just deciding something is bad, it is about sentencing anything within duality: right or wrong, black or white, good or bad. That dynamic distracts us from the real issue of being love in each and every moment. On the path of spiritual initiation, judgment causes us to continually energise a sense of self-righteousness, spiritual pride and the illusion of important work. Judgment is icy and heartless. It creates heaviness, and pulls the consciousness out of our heart centre into the lower chakras. The more we judge, the more heaviness, condition and limit we create. If we pursue judgment deep enough, we create despair and hopelessness. It creates a feeling of being anchored and disempowered, instead of joyous. Joy has a freedom from judgment associated with it, a lightness and limitlessness.

Judgement is a choice and an activity. It is something you choose to do and put energy into. In the same way, you can choose non-judgment and put your energy into being love, compassion and joy. It is not about denying the existence of your judgment, but about acknowledging it, stopping it, ceasing this activity, and then releasing the value judgment you have been holding on to.

Release the judgment and exercise radical, total forgiveness and tolerance. It may be of oneself, an ex-lover, boss, parent, guru, stepfather, stepmother, stepbrother or sister, a sibling, a place, a time, an idea, world events or an object.

It all just is.

"I choose to grow. In my intention to grow, I accept the truth, so that I can allow that which needs to be felt, integrated, transmuted and released"

Step 8. Re-choose

The old paradigm is about fear and control. We know about fear and suffering, and we don't have to suffer to be holy. Source does not want you to suffer. Choose the new, even if you don't know specifically what the new is. We do know the new is about love and joy. Whatever 'new' you choose, make sure you feel it and know it to be real as it comes forth from within you.

The law of magnetic attraction is one of the immutable laws of this world: like attracts like. The future is not something that we move into; it is something that we draw and attract into our now moments. The only time we can – or should – ever be is in the now.

Through our choices we set up circumstances, in every moment, magnetically drawing our future. We must own that we create everything we experience. If we adopt any victim consciousness, we can only create a fragment, at best, of our goal and purpose.

All fear we experience is the sum-total of the choices we have made - on our journey through eternity - to avoid and deny the truth. Each time we have a choice of love or fear and we choose the fear vibration by avoiding, denying, judging and experiencing fear - not being our best - we are effectively shutting down our capacity to love.

From the heart, choose to resonate with a heart-Mastery (Sacred Consciousness) quality (see 'Harmonise' step for examples of such energies).

"I choose to release fear, judgment and illusion; to be love. I give permission and authority not to an external force, but to the Spiritual Source within me."

"I am the cause of my attitudes, feelings, emotions and behaviour. I realise that every situation provides an opportunity to learn and grow. I now choose to recognise that I deserve love, and so do other people."

Step 9. Release

To allow our re-choosing to anchor and fill us with its new-ness, we need to make space for it. Allow any pattern or energy which no longer serves to be released and removed completely from your system. If it no longer serves, then you no longer need it. Let go of any attachment or illusion of need around the issue, feeling, the situation or people involved. Do not waste time or energy re-engaging with the old, which no longer serves you. Don't think about it. Simply let it go as you focus on and embrace the wonder of your new choice, with upcast eyes and a heart filled with hope. Let go of any attachment or preconceptions about who you are or should be, or what you can or can't do. Allow the Source within to create its own knowing, and have trust in that.

Once you have released the judgment, there is nothing keeping the old energy trapped in your system. As you allow the new choice to be felt and to become real, you are committed to letting go of anything within your system which does not agree with your new choice. Step into the new; and for this the old needs to be returned to its home in space-time.

"I choose to release all that no longer serves me"

"I release this energy, which is not of me, and return it to its original source."

Step 10. Harmonise

Allow the new chosen sacred quality - or energy of unconditional love and above - to fill any place or space within you and the planet around you. Allow the new chosen quality to replace anything you are releasing. Become it, embody it, be it and live it. Some examples of Sacred qualities are hope, openness, belief, aspiration, truth, intuition, discernment, curiosity, loyalty, humility, knowing, honesty, integrity, charm, worthiness, courage, gratitude, unity, wisdom, flow, innocence, joy, serenity, patience, adaptability, illumination, mercy, harmony, compassion and acceptance.

Feel the power of love moving through you and restoring balance. Expand it within your entire being, ground it and make it real. This is who you choose to be, this is how you choose to express now. See it, feel it and know it. Allow the change to ripple out throughout your entire life, and your entire sphere of influence. If you have truly embraced the process, you will feel a drive to change your behaviour and/or way of being as a result.

"I choose pure awareness, true consciousness, self mastery and authenticity, I choose, I AM"

If you but choose then, *Welcome HOME.*

http://mysteryschool.org.au

Conclusion

~~~

Crystals have always fascinated us. Throughout the ages, those who "know" have used Quartz crystals in their quest to re-unite humanity with its divine Source. Crystals have long been used as a trusted window into other realms of consciousness, to alter and enhance perception, to unlock spiritual illumination, and to promote spiritual and physical wellbeing. Working with crystalline energies assists us to align and activate our spiritual abilities, so that we may realise who we really are, and truly begin to live our lives free from the chains of a closed mind and heart. There is a complete absence of avoidance and denial in the mineral kingdom, which is why the great sages of history have so often strongly encouraged us to work with them. Crystals help us to consciously open our hearts to the possibility of loving unconditionally, without expectation of return.

Love is All, All is love,
Beyond All is Love and
Loving All is the Beyond ......

www.ingramcontent.com/pod-product-compliance
Lightning Source LLC
Chambersburg PA
CBHW032012080426
42735CB00007B/588